Lagrasse
and the Corbières

Lagrasse
and the Corbières

Life in the deep south of France

Stuart Benton

Published by CreateSpace

ISBN 978-1-977- 92940-2

Book formatted by www.bookformatting.co.uk.

Contents

ACKNOWLEDGEMENTS

A huge thank you to Barry Lewis for providing so many of the excellent photographs and to Hannah Charlton for her impeccable advice.

To my wife, children, family, friends
and the wonderful people of Lagrasse
who have made our time here so special.

Jewel of the Corbières

Ah Lagrasse! Le plus beau village de France!
Nestled in the hills of the Corbières,
A precious jewel set in emerald green,
Blessed by earth's crystal clear healing waters
Where tiny fish glide over smooth white stone
And children swim in sun-drenched innocence.
Opalescent luminescence dapples
The length and breadth of the Promenade
Highlighting the silver-grey and earth-grey
Dual-shaded bark of myriad plane trees
Resplendent and smooth as lapis lazuli.
Pink and ruby wine flow freely under
A perfect Mediterranean sky;
Diamond white in a sapphire blue surround.

Potters and painters, sculptors and vintners
Line ancient medieval cobbled streets
That lead the traveller unhurriedly
To the ageless Benedictine abbey
Whose cloisters and galleries still resound
With the ghostly footsteps of worshippers
Wandering forever in Time, searching
For Truth and Beauty or God's sublime Love.
Above the silhouette of the Pyrenees,
Eagles coast the knife blade painted garrigue,
While across the river, two old stone
Vaulted bridges arc through the air like doves
Leaving perfect loops in space, reflected
In the cool water's translucent mirror.

Stuart Benton

"Every book is, in an intimate sense, a circular letter to the friends of him who writes it. They alone take his meaning; they find private messages, assurances of love, and expressions of gratitude, dropped for them in every corner. The public is but a generous patron who defrays the postage. Yet though the letter is directed to all, we have an old and kindly custom of addressing it on the outside to one. Of what shall a man be proud, if he is not proud of his friends?"

Robert Louis Stevenson – 'Travels with a Donkey in the Cévennes'

And indeed there will be time
To wonder

T.S. Eliot – The Love Song of J. Alfred Prufrock

In memory of Henry Blackmore

ROUILLÉ, ROUILLÉ GOOD!

Lagrasse

Where to start? I am sitting in the kitchen of our recently purchased French house drinking ice cold rosé wine to the strains of an old Simon and Garfunkel album whilst my wife Sue heats up a take-away seafood paella. I could have bought take-away moules marinière, bouillabaisse, home-made fish soup, or even zarzuela (a traditional Catalan seafood stew) from the Poissonnerie in the nearby town of Lézignan-Corbières on our way home from the Lac de Taurize where my family spent the day swimming, jumping twenty feet off the rocks and drying off in the blazing August sunshine.

As it happens, I did also buy the fish soup. The vendor even threw in some biscottes, grated cheese and rouillé: a garlicky creamy topping for the biscottes which bob on top of the soup enhancing the whole experience. Our eldest son, Jon, said it was "rouillé, rouillé good" which made us all laugh.

Now that I've got the first of many ever-so upper-middle class "Living in France" bons mots over with, I feel ready to offer you, gentle reader, the chance to indulge your senses from afar, to dip a toe in the cool, clear rivers of the Occitanie; to get a taste of this region's mouth-watering gastronomy and to be caressed by the incredible sensation of experiencing what it is like to enjoy living in France – or as a friend here so poetically phrased it – "doing gentle nothingness".

We live in the south-west of France in the 'département' called the Aude, hidden away in the hills of the Corbières, half an hour from the cities of Carcassonne and Narbonne, and close to the Mediterranean Sea in the medieval village of Lagrasse. The French tourist board has classed Lagrasse as "one of the most beautiful villages in France". Time stands still in this extraordinary place; it is a medieval marvel, replete with cobbled streets, golden stone houses and quiet squares. It has an abbey commissioned in the 8th century by Charlemagne which overlooks the river Orbière where, during the summer months, villagers young and old swim in the crystal clear waters. Two old stone bridges span the river and give access to the garrigue[1] and the green hills beyond.

There were many reasons for choosing to buy a house in this particular village such as the easy access to the river for swimming and the fact that there are half a dozen places to eat within the village itself. During the day, we can not only saunter out of our

---

[1] Garrigue refers to the low-growing vegetation on the limestone hills of the surrounding area. There are many fragrant plants that grow wild here, such as rosemary, lavender, juniper and thyme. According to one of our friends "the most wonderful honey in the world" is made here where the bees produce many different flavours depending on which plants they feed on.

front door and be on the small pebble beach in less than a minute but also choose to dine out at any one of the excellent, friendly restaurants, and afterwards meander home through the tiny, cobbled streets.

Everything is on hand: we have the obligatory café, boulangerie/patisserie, tabac and pharmacie, as well as the Poste and the Mairie, which are both located in the central square known as the 'Place de la Halle'. This enchanting square, at the heart of the village, is enclosed by magnificent 14th and 15th century houses, with their wrought-iron balconies overlooking its very own medieval, open-air market hall. A wooden roof, supported by eight stone pillars, covers the large, shiny flag stones, polished and worn smooth over the centuries by countless passers-by.

Lagrasse – 8th century abbey commissioned by Charlemagne

Lagrasse is renowned for being an artists' village. We have potters, painters and sculptors who exhibit their art in quaint galleries, studios and shops throughout the village and along the Promenade, as well as an abundance of musicians who often appear out of nowhere to serenade us with trumpet, soprano saxophone and guitars, playing in the restaurants, outside the vintner's outlets or even on the beach at night. The abbey hosts cultural events during the year such as the internationally renowned book and philosophy fair "Le Banquet du Livre", classical music concerts and even once hosting a performance by dancers from the Royal Ballet.

What's more, Lagrasse is just forty minutes from the Mediterranean coast with its oyster bars, pink flamingo lagoons ("étangs" in French) and luxurious sandy beaches that stretch for miles and miles. Peppered along the coastline, there are many hip and stylish beach bars and restaurants serving an abundance of fish and seafood in a relaxed, informal setting which we often visit in the company of friends. We've had some great parties here! Inland, there is a huge choice of restaurants in the nearby villages and towns from old fashioned bistros and lunchtime cafés to crêperies and even a Michelin star restaurant. Obviously it goes without saying that a trip to France, and especially the Occitanie, is a gastronomic delight. Oh yes…and the wine is very cheap as well.

ROUILLÉ, ROUILLÉ GOOD!

In the Corbières, you are surrounded by vines on all sides wherever you go. Green and luscious in the spring and summer, the vines turn gold, red and orange in the autumn adding unforgettable, breath-taking splashes of colour to the fields and hillsides. Wine production is the major industry in the larger Occitanie and it is said to be the single biggest wine-producing region in the world, with output greater than that of Australia and the USA. The Corbières, as well as being the name given to the range of hills before the Pyrenees begin, is its largest wine AOC (Appellation d'Origine Contrôlée) with a variety of soil types and microclimates. The AOC Corbières stretches from Carcassonne in the north-west to Narbonne and Leucate on the coast, from the Black Mountains to the foothills of the Pyrenees in the south, covering an area of 11,800 hectares. The most famous local grape varieties ("cépages" in French) that go to make the red wine here are Carignan, Grenache and Cinsault; Syrah and Mourvèdre have also been used in recent times to boost quality and give the wine more body. For the whites the most common grape varieties are Maccabeu, Grenache blanc, Clairette and Terret (which is grown extensively around the port of Marseillan, home of French vermouth).

For us, the best of all has to be one of the oldest Languedoc grapes, the Piquepoul, which produces the crisp, dry Picpoul de Pinet wine – absolutely delicious when accompanied by oysters from Bouzigues, literally a stone's throw from where it is made. To finish off a traditional French meal in style, the versatile Muscat cépage is a treat. It used to be grown exclusively for vin doux naturel (sweeter wines) such as Saint Jean de Minervois and Rivesaltes but also serves as an excellent ice-cold aperitif and even produces full-flavoured dry wines as well.

The region is also justifiably famous for its ancient castles and they make for a great day out combined with a picnic or a simple 'plat du jour' lunch at one of the neighbouring village cafés. The most well-known castles are Carcassonne, Aguilar, Termes, Montségur, Lastours, Peyrepertuse and Queribus. Some of these are situated in remote mountainous areas and are best explored on less windy days as they are unsurprisingly built on higher ground. They were all used as temporary refuges in the 13th century by the Cathars, a religious sect of Gnostic Christians, when Pope (not-so) Innocent III called for a Catholic crusade to wipe them from the face of the earth…and he succeeded! Burnt alive by the hundreds, slaughtered by the thousands, maimed, disfigured and tortured, the poor Cathars were unceremoniously exterminated, with the atmospheric castle at Montségur in the Ariege region being the last stronghold to fall after nearly a whole year of siege in 1244. More on this gruesome history in a later chapter, but for now let us leave 'the good Christians' to their sad fate and allow me to wax lyrical on how we came to be living in the heart of the Corbières, France's most beguiling and charismatic region.

Lagrasse

HOUSE HUNTING

For our family, the number one priority when looking to buy a house in France, was the weather. Much of England's green and pleasant countryside is extremely beautiful, but only because it rains so much! Ideally we wanted a contrast to our life in England and also to be able to go swimming every day. So when considering which area of France to choose we wanted plenty of sunshine, clean rivers and proximity to the sea.

I was advised that anywhere south of Limoges, the weather is consistently hotter and drier than elsewhere in France. Even so, there are pockets of the south where it rains a great deal; like in the Cevennes, a range of mountains in south-central France made famous by Robert Louis Stevenson in his book "Travels with a

Donkey in the Cévennes", which cover parts of the départements of the Ardèche, Gard, Lozère and Hérault. This good advice led us to look even further south and so the Corbières and Aude region appealed above others as house prices and living costs were considerably more affordable than in Provence and the Cote d'Azur. People have christened the area "the other South of France" and as an alternative to the Cote d'Azur it has excellent credentials. The region's tourist offices never fail to miss an opportunity to stake the claim that "we have over 300 days of sunshine a year" which is clearly a positive sign. The Mediterranean Sea is just as warm and beautiful "round the bend" from Marseille so why pay between 25 and 50 percent more for everything and be hemmed in by too many tourists in expensive and showy glitterati resorts like Nice, Saint Tropez and Cannes? The beaches here with their golden sand are just as pretty as the ones in Provence with far less people on them.

Admittedly, we too have our strong winds similar to the Mistral that pummels the Cote d'Azur. There is the Tramontane wind which during the low season can be so ferocious, bombarding seaside towns like Collioure and Banyuls, it can literally send people mad. The dry Cers wind brings cold weather from the northwest while the Marin wind brings warm, humid air from the Mediterranean Sea. Before we make the journey to the coast for a day out on the beach, we always check the wind speed first. We have found that speeds of anything over 20 km/hour means that sunbathing on the beach is uncomfortable with the wind blowing sand in your face so we simply choose not to go on those days. During the year the coast plays host to world-renown windsurfing competitions, especially at Leucate, but of course this only adds to its many attractions. People comment when visiting this coastal region, especially in towns like Bouzigues as the sun sets on the horizon over the port of Sète in the distance or in the beautiful fishing village of Collioure where Matisse, Derain and the Fauvist art movement set up shop, that the unspoilt, sea-lined townships are more like those of the Cote d'Azur back in the 1920's and 1930's before commercialisation.

Collioure harbour

The way of life here is more relaxed and far less commercial than the topiary-obsessed Cote d'Azur with its chocolate box houses and endless tourists. Over recent decades, many artists have settled here in the Aude, attracted no doubt by cheaper living costs and the remoteness of the untamed Corbières with its mountain scenery, dramatic gorges and, most especially, the extraordinary translucent light to work by. There is a more "hippy", laid back ambience to the area; in fact the colloquial term for the down-to-earth people of the locality is, in French slang: "roots"! Moreover, for us, the Mediterranean Sea lies in striking distance of most villages and there are many rivers and lakes to swim in.

We started searching for a house at least five years before actually finding the right one, trawling the internet in our spare time at home in England. The estate agent photographs of French houses for sale with their higgledy-piggledy rooms, dilapidated outbuildings and scruffy patches of land were absolutely hilarious. It was as if vendors were trying their utmost to put people off buying them! Even when more than just two or three photos were available on the estate agent's website, it seemed obligatory to show as much clutter as possible strewn throughout the rooms of the houses. Photos showing kitchens with the shopping still in its plastic bags dumped on the table or bedrooms scattered with unwashed clothes and other debris were "de rigueur". Instead of presenting the properties from their best angles, the photographs would show dark and dingy rooms, crumbling masonry and unattractive surrounding scrubland. No wonder it can take years for houses to sell in France.

We had a number of near misses before finding the right house. The first property we visited was a lovely, old presbytery in a remote village in the Lauregais, a region renowned for its spectacular sunflower fields east of Carcassonne. Nearby Castelnaudry, situated on the Canal du Midi, is home to the infamous cassoulet: a rich, slow-cooked casserole containing Toulouse pork sausages, duck, pork skin (couennes) and white beans (haricots blancs).

Traditional Cassoulet

The house was very old and quite dark but with the gorgeous swimming pool at the back and wonderful views, we initially thought we could make a go of it. Fortunately for us, we had a survey performed on the house before making any decisions. When the surveyor's report came back, we couldn't believe what he had discovered: the king post in the attic was completely free from its anchor at the centre of the roof. The surveyor told us it was one for his nightmare picture gallery, his personal record of the very worst structural defaults he had encountered in his long career. The house would have required a brand new roof and we were simply not after such a big project. It would have been less costly for us had the vendor informed us of this "minor issue" when we were viewing the property.

The next house that we almost bought was actually located in the same village we are in now. As I have already stated, this particular village appealed to us for many reasons. It ticked all the boxes: river swimming literally on site, proximity to the beaches of the Mediterranean, its 8th century abbey, medieval streets and houses; the fact that it had a plethora of restaurants plus a café, boulangerie, tabac, poste, etc. I hopped on a plane and spent a weekend on a recce to make sure it was the right place for us.

When I was shown a traditional stone house by an estate agent, I was intrigued. We always referred to this property from then on as "the corner house" as it was wedged in the corner of an L-shaped street. It boasted many large rooms which would have been perfect for our big family and, of course, the obligatory illegal terrace on the roof, albeit of postage-stamp size. After much deliberation (and without really knowing if we could actually afford it), we made an offer to the German owners and thought an acceptance was imminent. However it was not to be. We were gazumped at the last minute by the Frenchman next-door!

I returned to England disheartened – all those years hunting for the right house only to fall at the last hurdle. Back in my study at home I switched on the computer and tried one more search on the internet and, as luck would have it, up popped a site offering a house in the same village for private sale. The house looked perfect from what I could tell from the photographs and was on offer at a reasonable price. I contacted the English owner who explained that after ten happy years in the house he now wanted the money to restore his boat in Chichester. I jumped on a plane and headed back within days and met the owner, a well-respected architect, and was given a tour of the property. He explained that he had restored the house entirely by himself and it was certainly evident that a skilled hand had been at work on the place. The interior was finished to a very high spec and the layout of the rooms suited us nicely. After the tour I told him straight out that I would like to offer the asking price, not even bothering to haggle. He was delighted and we shook hands there and then on the deal. It was only until I was on the plane back home, sipping a self-congratulatory glass of red wine, that I realised I had just bought a house in France without my wife ever having stepped foot in it! Fortunately, when they visited the place for the first time, my wife and children all loved the house as much as I did. So we eventually ended up buying a place in France without the aid of an estate agent, saving thousands of euros in fees (estate agents can take up to a whopping 10% of the value of the house as opposed to England's 1 %). Having said that, if you would like help in finding a house to buy in our area, the best agent is our friend Anna Stoloff whose website is www.homehunters france.com. Anna has helped hundreds of people find the perfect house in this neck of the woods.

Something we did want to ensure was that we were able to avoid the confusing (and potentially disastrous) antiquated French law that states that a property must be divided equally amongst the surviving children upon the demise of the owner. Surely an abject lesson in how to create chaos (although I can now confirm that this outmoded ruling was rescinded in August 2015, and only one law will apply from this date for all assets, whether movable or immovable, personal or real property: the law of your country of residence). At the time, however, it was clear this stipulation could not only cause rows amongst family members but also be very difficult to administrate. What if you had four children like us and they were all scattered around the globe? Worse still what if the children disagreed as to whether to keep or sell the property? We could see no positives in allowing the possibility of this happening and so on our next visit to the house – once we had legally taken ownership – my wife and I took a trip to a local notaire's offices and signed a special document called a "communauté universelle", by far the simplest method of ensuring that the house would be bequeathed only to the surviving spouse. The notaire's offices in the neighbouring village of Fabrezan were located in a beautiful old house with a huge courtyard built many years ago from the proceeds of the highly successful wine trade in the village. Finally we had done it – our own little slice of France.

CHEZ NOUS

As I have already mentioned, our house is a small pied-a-terre in a beautiful, medieval village with its cobbled streets, quiet squares, Benedictine abbey and very own river beach. Officially classed as "one of the most beautiful villages in France" it enjoys a great deal of sunshine and it is often possible to dine outside wearing only t-shirt and shorts in December. Nestled in the foothills of the wild Corbières, the village is just 40 minutes from the Mediterranean sea.

We still do not know exactly how old the house is. Estimates from neighbours range from 17th, 18th or 19th century (take your pick!) and it is built from local stone. We have named the house "La

Maison du Berger Constant" because early in the 20th century it belonged to a local shepherd, Monsieur Constant, who would leave the village each year in spring to tend his flock in the Pyrenees and return to the house in time for winter. The old French lady on the Promenade, with whom I gossip in the mornings, can still remember him. The view out of the front of the house from all three floors is of the gorgeous "rue du pech" dappled in sunlight with bright flowers and plants outside the houses; all under the canopy of a deep, azure blue Mediterranean sky.

View of the street from our front door

15

Most houses in the village have either a courtyard within or behind the house and/or a "terrasse" on the roof (90% are illegal but that doesn't stop the French). For us, the compromise we made when buying the house was to make do with very little outside space. However, we do have a wooden bench set into the wall out front to sit on and play guitar to the passers-by. We have both classical and acoustic guitars in the house with which to serenade them. There is a small metal grate set in the wall by the seat which our ultra-friendly French neighbour, Hervé, tells us was used to clean the fish caught in the river when he was a boy.

Marie-Claude with an extremely tasty 'Couronne d'agneau'

Hervé was born in the village and the house opposite has been in his family for more than six generations. Formerly Production Director of Renault at their main manufacturing plant in Lille, he oversaw thousands of workers and dealt with one or two strikes in his time. He and his charming wife Marie-Claude have now retired here and both play an active role in the village's many activities. Marie-Claude attends a great deal of the literature and poetry lectures held in the abbey and Hervé is a keen wild boar hunter, "vendangeur" (grape picker during the September harvest) and allotment keeper. The allotments here are very popular and run the length of the river to the side of the abbey. It is from here that Hervé produces a bewildering array of vegetables and fruit: huge sun-drenched tomatoes, cucumbers like javelins, red onions as big as discuses, courgettes, beetroot and the juiciest figs; the list is endless. He often very kindly leaves a kilo or three of each variety on the bench outside our house just for us.

Our neighbours' house itself is deceptively Tardis-like with elegant drawing rooms, a hidden courtyard (comprising an impressive stone barbeque) and an old half-moon shaped cellar that Hervé has converted into a splash pool. Many of the houses here are exquisitely renovated, decorated and furnished throughout; each one a delightful surprise when you are fortunate enough to be invited in. No one house is the same, dating as they do from the 14th century.

Although our own little house is old, the interior is furnished with all mod cons and the mix of old and new works perfectly for us. On the ground floor, we have an open plan living room / dining room / kitchen. We have a dining table which can seat four to six people comfortably, an easy-to-use gas fire in the style of a wood burner housed in a large fireplace beneath a mantelpiece made from reclaimed English oak by the previous owner and two comfortable armchairs by the fire. With wireless broadband internet connection throughout the house, not only can I work from here in the same way that I work from home in England but in addition the children can use their various iPhones/iPads/iPods when on holiday.

Open plan living room

Kitchen

We have some jazzy Bose speakers in the corner into which we take it in turns to dock our individual iPods so we can have a variety of music playing. Particularly useful when I'm out here on my own is a radio player app on my iPhone through which I can listen to Radio 3, 4 or 6 and also the BBC World Service (what expat wannabe could live without it?). The walls, shelves and mantelpiece are adorned with colourful pottery and paintings, all by local artists.

Upstairs on the first floor we have a spacious master bedroom and, off the landing, a shower room which includes the obligatory "bidet" or "bum-bath" as my youngest daughter Grace has re-christened it (I personally still believe to this day that the French wash their elbows in them, as my Dad once explained, presumably to save my Mum's blushes). Electric convectors heat all the rooms and the landing is illuminated by another example of local craftwork: a delightful, circular night lamp made entirely from white pebbles salvaged from the nearby river.

Master bedroom

Covering the whole of the top floor is a large second bedroom, this time with three double beds for the children. The room has a Narnia-style wardrobe which you have to climb up into and which doubles as much-needed storage space. I also have a desk, telephone and printer in the corner so that I can work from here with ease.

And that's it. Compact and bijou, as Stephen Fry would say.

Top floor bedroom

RAISONS D'ÊTRE (ICI)

My own personal love affair with France began way back when I was twelve years old. The only reason I can now converse fluently in French (does anyone truly speak any language fluently?) is due to the kindness of my parents; they organised exchange visits for me with French families every summer throughout my school years. I can still remember holding the hand of a British Airways stewardess as she accompanied me on board the plane for my first trip to the Gendrot family home on the outskirts of Paris back in 1977. It didn't occur to me to be nervous or worried. I innocently believed it was perfectly normal to be a child travelling alone to a foreign country.

The Gendrots had three children: Hervé, Pascal and Claire.

Hervé was my age so he became my first French friend and we spent the next three summers either in Paris or Wolverhampton (what a culture shock that must have been for him). His whole family were very kind to me and I didn't miss home at all. Hervé and I were both keen numismatists, that is to say, coin collectors, and I remember buying my first Napoleon III silver coin at one of the stalls next to the old book vendors on the banks of the river Seine in central Paris. Everything was an adventure to me and I soon picked up the lingo (because if you want to buy sweets and coins, then you are obliged to ask for them). It was a perfect way to learn the language.

We didn't just stay in Paris. Hervé's father worked for the French government and was involved in politics in some capacity so they weren't short of a few francs. As a result they owned a house by the sea in Fromentine near the Isle of Noirmoutier in the Vendée on the west coast and also a huge country house in the remote countryside somewhere in the middle of France (I was just too young to remember precisely where geographically the country house was located). Each summer we would spend several weeks at one or the other. From Paris the whole family (including their dog) would up sticks and travel to the coast so that we could swim in the sea, play pétanque on the gravelled courts by the shore or collect tiny shrimp (crevettes in French) at dawn on the beach, catching them in our little nets dangled on the end of a long stick. Hervé's Mum prepared these for our lunch on the same day and they were eaten fresh on baguettes with salted butter – delicious. They had a big, lolloping dog called Milord, and when Hervé's mother made pasta for us she would always give the dog the same food. At mealtimes, I remember being amazed that the children were offered glasses of red wine diluted with water – unheard of back home.

On the subject of food, it was in Fromentine that I first tried frogs' legs. I have to hand it to them, the family invented a great ruse to get me to eat what I'm pretty sure I would have refused had I been told what I was really eating: they told me they were "petits oiseaux" or "little birds"! The family only let on that they were, in fact, frogs' legs after I'd devoured my second helping. Actually, when cooked properly they taste just like sweet chicken (I now know from experience that when cooked badly they taste like frogs' legs!). Snails in garlic butter were my other favourite (I must have been a Frenchman in a past life). In the Vendée, the locals used to drive out at night to a secluded road, leave their car headlights on and wait for the snails to slowly cross the tarmac, then pick them all up and put them in a basket to take home.

The trips to the family's house in the countryside were straight out of Swallows and Amazons. At the bottom of the huge garden was a wide stream and they had diverted some of the water to form a miniature, man-made lake complete with its own islands and narrow waterways which we would navigate using small kayaks; we spent endless hours playing there. I can't remember a great deal about the country house itself except for the ginormous fireplace in the main hall – you could get a bus through there.

In later summers, when the Gendrot family chose to stop sending Hervé on any more exchange trips, they very kindly put my parents in touch with their cousins in Landernau, which is near Brest in Brittany, and I spent the summer there when I was sixteen. Their son was called Thierry: a tall, gangly teenager with a permanent wispy stubble on his chin and a twenty-a-day habit of smoking foul smelling Gauloises and Gitanes cigarettes. I remember his feet stank as he would wear the same socks every day! Despite his malodourous peccadilloes he became a great friend and I first learned to play the guitar because of him. I remember that year we went camping with his family and stayed on one of those ubiquitous French campsites set in pine tree forests. The night sky was pitch black because there was very little artificial light and consequently filled with thousands of stars every night, including literally scores of shooting stars. I remember vividly when one of the French ground staff, who by day looked after the tennis courts, played the entire solo of Hotel California by the Eagles on his guitar one evening to an audience of just three of us. Very impressive. I also remember fondly the many different concoctions that the bar staff used to serve up: "exotic" drinks like "diablo" (mint syrup and lemonade), "perroquet" (pastis and mint syrup with lots of ice) and "tomate" (pastis and grenadine).

The following summer, when I was seventeen, was not the garden of roses that the previous ones had been. Thierry's family stopped their exchange visits so I eventually hooked up with a French lad who was attending my school in England at the time. Frederick was an absolute nightmare: over excited, constantly getting into trouble at school and we eventually came to the conclusion that he must have been either schizophrenic or bi-polar such were his violent mood swings. I spent some time at his family's Paris flat and a wonderful day at their Grandmother's country home where my parents joined us for a memorable 6 hour lunch but unfortunately the memory that endures most vividly was when his family took me on a skiing trip to Austria during the winter of that year. Although accompanied by Frederick, his older brother Valérie (tricky name for a boy had he been English), their sister Emmanuelle and strange father and cranky mother, I was made to feel very much alone. Around the breakfast table in the hotel one morning, the day after one of the parents' pensioner friends had lent me his ski pass for some reason or other, I was accused by the mother of abusing my trust with the old man and being a liar! Charming. That evening, following a game of table football in the basement of the hotel and in response to my winning the game, Frederick proceeded to thump me very hard on the nose from across the table! Blood gushed like a fountain from my flattened hooter all over the floor as I in turn chased him round the room trying in vain to thump him back. Later that night when he, Valérie and I were in our beds in our shared room, his brother proceeded to level taunts and cruel threats at me making me feel very lonely and quite frightened. Obviously not my best Francophile memory.

Well, what doesn't kill you makes you stronger, as they say, and I wasn't about to tar all French people with the same brush just because of a few altercations with a bunch of nutters, so in the summer of 1981, when I was eighteen and waiting to start my Humanities degree (majoring in French and English), I took up an offer from an American friend of our English neighbour to go and work for a couple of months in a Foyer des Jeunes in Montparnasse, Paris. Similar to a Youth Hostel, but temporarily acting as a seasonal hotel for visiting American tourists, it was located off the main boulevard near Denfert-Rochereau metro station. Crammed full of young people from around the world, it was an exciting and vibrant place to be. My job, and that of my fellow worker Jake, also from England, was to chaperone and act as guide for the American tourists showing them round the usual haunts of the Latin Quarter, Saint-Germain des Prés (with its famous cafés like Les Deux Magots which Sartre, Picasso and other famous writers/artists used to frequent); the Louvre, Notre Dame, the Eiffel Tower, etc. etc.. When the Americans arrived in their all-new, air-conditioned coaches, I would jump on board, grab the microphone, and warmly welcome them all to Paris and the Foyer. They were a nice crowd, with the exception of one or two oddballs, like the racist South Carolinians who were unimpressed by the many North Africans working in the Foyer. I remember escorting one family on the metro to their Consulate after their wallet and passport went missing as they huddled together on the train, holding on to each other for dear life, paranoid and scared out of their wits by the multi-cultural mix of fellow commuters. Way over the top. Life was fun for me working at the Foyer and time off was spent at the Café Saint-Jacques, just down the way on the corner of our street, where I spent long afternoons shooting pool and listening to Ray Charles on the jukebox over a cold pastis or two.

Some years later, due to the fact I had opted for what was then called a sandwich course, the third year of my degree was to be spent studying at the Université de Lyon. Known as the gastronomic capital of France (but then I'm sure there are plenty of other candidates for the accolade in a country renowned for its cuisine), Lyon had a village feel to it even though it's France's third largest city after Paris and Marseille. The two rivers, the Rhone and the smaller, prettier Saône, converge to the south of the historic city centre forming a peninsula or "Presqu'île". Flanked by busy quartiers or arrondissements like Saint Jean, Saint Paul and Saint George in Vieux Lyon (the old town), Bellecour, Terreaux and

Perrache; with the slopes of the Croix-Rousse and the Roman foundation at Fourvière hill overlooking everything.

Not being the world's most focused student, I turned up at the university on the first day, attended one hour's lecture and never went again. Rather, I spent the year either partying or working as a barman in English and Irish pubs that had only recently sprung up in Lyon (now to be found in every French city whether you like them or not), alternately living in small, one-bed flats – like the one off Boulevard Victor Hugo from where I had to make a timely escape after the purportedly 'middle-class professional', from whom I was renting the room, went on a heroin-induced rampage, smashing his flat up in the process, and various squats with new-found friends. In one of the squats lived an artist: a gentle soul named Paul, whose work at the time consisted entirely of photographs of people's faces with their eyes closed, which had the surprising effect of making them all look serenely happy and contented. There were plenty of other characters dossing in the squat, like the jovial Babbas and his skinny girlfriend, whose chief method of survival was shoplifting in order to eat. Well, you've got to eat, haven't you? I have happy memories of laughing a lot and drinking gallons of wine with these new, transient friends.

I lived for a time in a cool flat on the side of a local politician's house on the slopes of the superbly named Montée du Gourguillon in Saint George in the oldest part of town where Steve (a fellow student from Middlesbrough) and I would, to the amusement of our French guests, host all-night parties wearing (I have no idea why) dressing gowns and slippers (very Noel Coward) much to the chagrin of the politician next door who called the police on us one night: they turned up, took one look, laughed heartily and just drove away.

Incredibly, the following year, upon completing my degree back in England, they gave me a 2.2 grade which was known at the time, rather aptly, as a "drinkers' degree". Once I had finished my degree, having enjoyed my adventures in Lyon so much, I chose to return there for another year of youthful exuberance. This time I returned to the University and took a job as a teacher of English grammar to the French degree students at Lyon II (Faculté des Lettres). This betokened me 250 Francs for just thirteen hours work a week, enough to pay for rent on an open-plan flat, which boasted an amazing sunken bedroom accessed through a wide arch that looked like an upside down half-moon, somewhere on the slopes of the Croix-Rousse, and copious quantities of booze which I lavished on my guests at parties I gave in my funky new flat. A mix of students, lecturers, painters (including Jim Leon, the dreamscape painter), artists, junkies and squatter friends meant the parties were at the very least 'interesting'. In the evenings I worked at Le Cornishman Pub just down the road with an old English mate Dave and his French wife Katie where we showed the French how to drink pints of Guinness and play darts to the accompaniment of Ry Cooder and Jimi Hendrix. Dave and Katie had a fantastically scruffy dog, a randy red setter called George who used to take off on his own for days at a time and return completely bedraggled, covered in dirt and grime and God knows what, having presumably impregnated half of the city's unfortunate female dog population.

I returned to England at the age of twenty-three and the following year married my beautiful wife. Ever since I have worked in import/export and eventually started my own agency called SBS International Ltd. (est. 1994) working ostensibly with French companies to make the best use of my language abilities and my unremitting desire to return to 'La Douce France' as often as possible. I have since travelled all over France on business and would one day like to buy a ten bedroom farmhouse so that (if we're really lucky) all our children and grandchildren can come and stay with us. Hmm…going to need a swimming pool then.

THE LANGUEDOC-ROUSSILLON

The old Languedoc-Roussillon

It used to be straight-forward explaining to friends back home whereabouts in France the Corbières region was located: I would simply tell them it was in the "Languedoc-Roussillon". Dead easy. If they wanted to know where the Languedoc-Roussillon was, I would explain it was round the bend from the bustling port of

Marseille, chasing the Mediterranean Sea all the way down to the Spanish border and the Pyrenees mountains. If they wanted still more detail, I might have informed them that the Languedoc-Roussillon is a large administrative region of France comprising five 'départements': Lozère, Gard, Hérault, Aude and Pyrénées-Orientales. And if they were foolish enough to enquire further, I may have apprised them that the Lozère includes the Lot valley, the Gorges du Tarn and the northern part of the Cévennes; the Camargue (western Europe's largest river delta) and the south Cévennes make up the département of the Gard which borders the river Rhône and includes the city of Nimes, famous for its Roman Coliseum (second only to that of Rome) and its controversial bull fighting festivals. The Mediterranean coast, Haut-Languedoc and Minervois cover the départements of Hérault and the Aude, which also include the wild Corbières and the Montagne Noire. Finally, next to the Spanish border, Roussillon, the Vermilion coast and the Catalonian Pyrenees make up the Pyrénées-Orientales. That would usually shut them up.

However, just when I thought I'd got my bearings, all this changed in December 2015 when the French authorities decided to merge the Languedoc-Roussillon with a further eight neighbouring départements (collectively known as the Midi-Pyrénées) and so for six months the area was re-christened, somewhat maladroitly, as 'Languedoc-Roussillon-Midi-Pyrénées'. As this was understandably too much of a mouthful for the locals to swallow, the authorities in their wisdom chose to spend a mere half a million euros organising a vote for a more appropriate name. Anyone who owned a house in the region was eligible to vote for an abridged designation and on Friday 24th June 2016, the Regional Council authorised the new name: 'Occitanie'. This new name (pronounced "ock-sit-anny") is not a new name. Traditionally the whole swathe of the south of France, from the Atlantic coast to parts of eastern Italy, down to the Mediterranean coastline and even a part of northern Spain, was the true, historic Occitanie. This larger expanse shared a common language with no less than six different dialects; it was called the 'langue d'Oc' and is still spoken today.

The new Occitanie

As a consequence of the merger, the new Occitanie now covers a total area of over 28,000 square miles (nearly the size of Belgium with almost half as many inhabitants) and includes the new areas of Ariège, Aveyron, Gers, Haute-Garonne, Hautes-Pyrénées, Lot, Tarn and Tarn-et-Garonne making it the second largest region of France with Toulouse as the its capital (or 'préfecture' in French) and the whole boasting a total population of around six million people. At the same time, other regions of France were re-designated and restructured in a similar way and so now France is comprised of just thirteen regions in total. Of course, after all that, the French authorities just couldn't resist muddying the waters further and have chosen to add to the new name of our region 'Occitanie', the subtitle 'Pyrénées-Méditerranée'. This was to attempt to unify the French Catalans who might have objected to having their beloved Catalonia left out of the fun. At time of writing, Catalonia in its entirety describes a large part of north-eastern Spain including Barcelona but also a section of south-west France which forms a triangle between the Pyrenees to the south, the Corbières to the

30

north-west and the Mediterranean Sea to the east. Its principal French city is Perpignan. The renaming of our region has posed a considerable conundrum for me because when I began writing about this area, I officially lived in the 'Languedoc'. Now that I live in 'Occitanie-Pyrénées-Méditerranée' I am delighted to have been presented with a much larger geographical expanse to explore and experience.

There is a such a rich diversity of historical and cultural heritage in this part of France from the many rock caves like the Giant Chasm of Cabrespine, the Arago Cave at Tautavel where the bones discovered are among the oldest human remains ever to be found in Europe and the Niaux cave that houses 12,000 year old prehistoric paintings; to the uninvited Visigoth invaders of the early centuries of the first millennium and on to the outrageous crusading Catholics and hapless Cathars of the 12th and 13th Centuries with their famous castles and romantic troubadours. The Romans also left their mark in no uncertain terms building not just roads, arenas, viaducts, aqueducts and the odd temple but also ensuring the cities all have a common feel and flavour deriving from the layout of their streets and houses. Although the first vines in this area were said to have been planted by the early Greeks in the 5th century BC, a mere two thousand years ago the Romans added to the pot by planting countless vines here which are now the most common sight when travelling through the region.

Naturally, the authentic cuisine based on olive oil, garlic and basil, typically flavoured with herbs of the garrigue such as rosemary, bay or thyme, lend the area its most enduring aspect and cultural identity. Honey here is naturally flavoured by the bees who feed on the herbs in the hills (our local rosemary honey has been famous since Roman times); fruit and nut trees like figs, apricots and almonds are plentiful. Mushroom varieties like the Cèpes and Giroles are widespread and, unsurprisingly, the region's innumerable array of cheeses abound. We've tried some fabulous local dishes that are synonymous with towns and cities where they were first cooked up like the cassoulet of Castelnaudry, Brandade de Nimes, Bourride de Sète and my favourite, the Thau basin oysters. The Thau Basin to the north-east of the region is celebrated for having the best oysters in the region (the "Etang" produces 8000 tons every year and provides France with 10% of its total oyster yield).

Thau basin oysters

Along the sandy coastline of the Mediterranean sea, which stretches as far as Argelès-sur-Mer before the wild, rocky headlands of the purple-tinged Côte Vermeille rise out of the sea, you can find a bewildering assortment of seafood such as mussels, sea snails, clams, cockles, cuttlefish, octopus, squid, lobster, crab and scallops, as well as the most common fresh fish like sea bass and sea bream. The Côte Vermeille is also famous for its great artists like Matisse and Picasso who once found inspiration in the ports of Collioure and Banyuls.

The world renown Canal du Midi cuts a swathe through the area from Sète on the Mediterranean to near Bordeaux in the far west. It was certainly one of the greatest feats of engineering and construction of the 17th century and is one of the oldest working canals in Europe. Built to facilitate the wheat trade, it took 12,000 workers fourteen years to construct its 150 miles of length. Now primarily used by tourists for recreation, one can sail on chartered boats, restaurant-boats, or even hotel barges. Many of you will recall the excellent BBC television series Rick Stein's French Odyssey when the ebullient chef set sail on the canal indulging in and enlightening his audience with the myriad delights of the regional cuisine. Modern day visitors and locals can now also enjoy fishing, rowing, canoeing, cycling, hiking and even roller-skating along the banks but it is mostly used by us foreigners, mainly Germans and Brits. You can choose to cycle the entire route from Sète to Bordeaux, if you feel the urge, taking in the many restaurants and amazing converted barges that are moored permanently along its banks, many of which have been turned into 'houses' and restaurants, with even the odd theatre to boot.

THE CORBIÈRES

Obviously, it would take me forever to detail all the sights and attractions of the vast Occitanie in one book and so I will be offering instead a more personal view of the places that I have come to know rather than force you to trawl through umpteen facts and figures that can, in any case, be found in many different guide books and websites. As I've already stated, we live in the Aude and, more precisely, the Corbières. The name Corbières comes from "cor" a pre-Celtic word meaning "rock" and "berre" from the River Berre which runs through the commune of Durban. The Corbières is the mountainous region located mainly in the Aude and partly in the Pyrénées-Orientales to the south. It is a place of outstanding natural beauty and one of the wildest areas of France with a very low population density so its natives are generally less well-off financially here than in other more congested areas of France. The main industries are viticulture and tourism so life here is more gentle and laid back than its busier near-neighbours. It is extremely picturesque and bursting with field upon field of vines alternating with garrigue, gorges, ravines, valleys, rivers, lakes, hills and mountainous countryside. The River Aude borders the Corbières to the west and north; to the south is the River Agly and to the east the Mediterranean Sea.

The eastern part of the Corbières with its many pink flamingo festooned Étangs (basins or lagoons in English) borders the sea and is called the Corbières Maritimes. It has its own distinctive climate and characteristic vegetation, which I am reliably informed is known as 'thermo-Mediterranean' vegetation. Along the coast you can take your pick from rough and ready tourist beach resorts like Narbonne Plage and Port-la-Nouvelle, where in summer the tattoo to teeth ratio is just too close to call for me, or choose instead to visit the delightful, old-fashioned fishing villages and resorts of Gruissan, la Franqui, Leucate, Peyriac-de-Mer and Bages to name but a few.

View from the quaint fishing village of Bages

Our "terroir" is dominated by the Montagne d'Alaric, along the Aude valley between Narbonne and Carcassonne. The mountain is named after the Visigoth King Alaric II who fought the Franks in the 5th century. On certain days, when a halo of cloud sits on top, the locals can be heard to expound that "Alaric porte son chapeau" (Alaric is wearing his hat). Local tradition has it that he left a great treasure buried in the caves beneath the mountain but unfortunately we haven't found it yet! One of our neighbouring villages, Saint-Laurent de la Cabrerisse, boasts Visigothic carvings in the entrance of the church and, in case you're visiting, the village is also home to the excellent winery 'Cellier des Desmoiselles' which produces one of the nicest rosé wines in the Corbières.

The new Occitanie is one of the largest French wine producing areas in terms of volume, and the best-known of its 'Appellations Controlées' is the Corbières. Our region enjoys ideal conditions for wine growing: the Mediterranean climate of dry, sunny and warm weather suits the vines perfectly. The grapes ripen well and quickly in this region, producing rich, full-bodied wines, often with a high alcohol content. The north-west wind, present throughout the year, allows the wine growers to avoid excessive chemical treatments and preserves the acidity. AOC Corbières produces over 74 million bottles of wine ever year, and although around ninety percent of the production is red wine, the whites and rosés are equally as enjoyable.

To the west of the Corbières in the "Haute Vallée", the excellent sparkling wines, Blanquette de Limoux and Crémant de Limoux, are ideal as aperitifs. The limestone and clay soil of the Limoux vineyards attracts bees and wildflowers, lending honeyed notes to the wines. Legend has it that, following a visit to the region, Dom Pérignon borrowed the idea of sparkling wine and then introduced it to the Champagne area, but there is no proof this is actually true. What is true, however, is that the region around Limoux was producing sparkling wines half a century before the Champagne region, and, of course, the wines cost considerably less.

The Corbières AOC consists of 11 terroirs: Montagne d'Alaric, Saint Victor, Fontfroide, Queribus, Boutenac, Termenès, Lézignan, Lagrasse, Sigean, Durban and Serviès. The Decree of 27 December 1985, laying down the rules for the production of Corbières AOC wines, defines the list of authorised grape varieties. For the reds: Carignan, Cinsault, Grenache noir, Lledoner pelut, Mourvèdre, Piquepoul noir, Syrah and Terret noir. For the whites: Bourboulenc, Clairette, Maccabeu, Marsanne, Muscat, Piquepoul, Roussanne, Terret Blanc, Vermentino or Rolle, and White Grenache. For all those interested, the website: www.20decorbieres.com (you have to say the French word for the number 20 out loud to enjoy the pun) offers travellers the chance to visit some of the Corbières vineyards and sample the fruits of 1,300 producers. The "Route des 20" has five thematic routes: The Route of the Étangs and the Sea, The

Route of the Cathars, The Route of Boutenac, The Route of the Alaric and The Route of Narbonne to Lézignan-Corbières. Wine tasting ('degustation de vins' in French) is a fun thing to do, as long as you can find a teetotal driver to ferry you from one vineyard to the next. You are normally offered a guided tour of the chateau and its cellars, followed by a wine tasting session at the end. Very pleasant.

Many of our local villages conceal hidden gems, like quaint squares with fountains, sleepy cafés and art galleries, that are simply not visible from their main through-road and all the villages have their individual claims to fame which can only be discovered by taking a detour and making a closer inspection of the place. In fact, the best advice I can give you when visiting the Corbières, is not to make the mistake of simply driving straight through, but instead park the car and take the time to go for a tour of each village on foot. Just head for the main square, which may be tiny, but is usually the heart of the village, where you might find a small café at which to stop and quench your thirst; or a boulangerie for those irresistible cakes and fruit tarts that France is so rightly famous for. Perhaps you'll happen across a bench near a pretty fountain for you to rest a while and take in the ambience. In this way you'll get a real feel for the villages as they are all unique. I remember stopping a while in Camplong d'Aude and was not only rewarded with the sight of a gorgeous, spring-fed fountain (albeit painted a rather garish green!) in the middle of the little square but also the village's very own chateau with its stone clock tower over the gateway which I would have missed had I not made the effort to explore the village on foot.

Many of our local Corbières villages are also worthy of note as the birth places of French poets. For instance, Moux is the birthplace of the poet Henry Bataille (1872 -1922) where his tomb is topped by a weird but funky skeletal statue; Floure is the birthplace of the poet Gaston Bonheur (1923-1980) who founded a surrealist magazine called Choc and was also the director of Paris-Match; Villar-en-Val is the birthplace of the poet Joseph Delteil (1894 -1978) where the 11th-century church is home to an exhibition of his work during the summer.

Fabrezan is the next village on from ours and has a museum dedicated to Charles Cros (christened somewhat extravagantly as Émile-Hortensius-Charles Cros), yet another local poet and humorous writer, but also famous as the inventor of the phonograph (or Paleophone as he called it), later to evolve into the gramophone and then the turntable or record player. Cros' device could record sounds, but just to put the record straight (please excuse the pun), Thomas Edison was, in fact, the first person to invent a phonograph that was able to reproduce the recorded sound. Cros was also known for pioneering photographs in colour. Funnily enough, he bears a striking resemblance to my friend Gus (pronounced "goose" in French) who owns and chefs for the village's excellent pizzeria – maybe they're related? I shall have to ask him. For more details on this famous inventor, please visit the website: www.fabrezan.fr.

Émile-Hortensius-Charles Cros

The villages of the Corbières are inexorably linked to its Cathar history, especially when the pope's crusade against the heretical Cathars was at its most despotic. The nearby village of Villerouge-Termenès, said to be the Mediterranean door to the High Corbières, is one such village. In the centre of the medieval settlement is an imposing castle with four towers where visitors can enjoy an audio-visual tour which focuses its narrative on its most famous occupant Guilhem Belibaste, the last Cathar Perfect (Perfect was the name given to ordained Cathars). The unfortunate Belibaste was burnt at the stake here in 1321. Our family spent an afternoon here during one summer holiday as I thought it might be interesting for the children to learn something of the region's gruesome history. I knew they were big fans of the brilliant TV series "Horrible Histories" so presumed the gory details would be right up their street. Sure enough on our way round the castle on the audio-visual tour, equipped with headphones and English versions of the recorded history, my wife and I caught sight of our son, who was sixteen at the time, walking round nodding and smiling and seemingly enjoying the whole experience only to find his headphones were in fact plugged into his iPod and he had actually been listening to the Stone Roses instead. So much for trying to educate the youth of today then.

Strictly speaking, the famous 'Cathar castles' of the Aude, known as the five sons of Carcassonne (namely Peyrepertuse, Quéribus, Puivert, Aguilar and Termes) can't truly be called Cathar castles, as the tourist offices would have us believe, because they were in fact built by the French Kings to protect their interests in the south of the country. Nevertheless they certainly acted as strongholds during the campaign sheltering hundreds of innocent Cathars during this diabolical period in history. Many of the powerful lords of the castles were predisposed to the Cathars and sympathetic to their plight, and so numerous 'Good Christians' took refuge in these stone fortresses from the brutal inquisition being waged without mercy by the pope's relentless Crusaders. For instance, in 1210, during the Albigensian Crusade, as it became known, the fortress of Termes held out for four months against the

Crusaders who were commanded by Simon de Montfort, the most vicious of all the pope's warlords. Termes is not far from our village and well worth a visit especially in summer when the local authorities put on a lively, medieval-themed pageant. At Termes, there's an incredible fresh water pool that mostly locals visit which has at least four jumping off places but be careful because it's pretty wild. I have heard the story of people jumping in to one of the many pools in the Corbières gorges and not being able to climb out again. No idea if that's true, but it would make for a great story!

Waterfalls and natural pool at Termes

WILD RIVER SWIMMING

Gorgeous!

Every year, during the summer months of July and August, we come to the house "en famille" to holiday so the whole family can swim and take full advantage of the glorious weather. Temperatures often hit the 90s and 100s (or if you're under 50 years old, the 30s and 40s). For me, temperatures in Fahrenheit are not just numbers for scientists but instead evoke memories and feelings. So, for instance, the words '70 degrees Fahrenheit' remind me of a perfect English summer's day: not too hot, not too cold. 80 degrees Fahrenheit and my mind travels to childhood holiday destinations like Majorca or Greece but 90 degrees Fahrenheit is the perfect temperature for river swimming in the south of France.

The most magical places to visit are indeed the river swimming spots all around us. Apart from the one in the village itself, there are innumerable places along the different rivers where you can park up and discover incredible hidden pools, tumbling waterfalls and paradisiacal stretches of clear water surrounded by nature on all sides. The waters are extremely clean, nearly as warm as the Mediterranean and so clear that you can see the smooth stones beneath your feet and the little fishes swimming by. We have spent many a sun-drenched afternoon with a picnic of baguettes, cheese and salads – accompanied by the obligatory bottle of wine – enjoying the peace and quiet of these magical places, often having the swimming spots all to ourselves. The locals keep the whereabouts of these hidden swimming spots a closely guarded secret until you ply them with a bottle of wine or two and then, if you're lucky, they might just let slip the location of one you haven't found yet!

Lagrasse beach and river

Swimming in the rivers, you are constantly reminded of the ever-changing nature of water: one moment it's warm, the next a refreshing coolness pervades. Your body revels in this natural impermanence and you remember you're a part of nature rather than a homogenised lump of 21st century automaton. In the rivers there are no smart phones, iPads, faxes or computers with their constant electronic bleating: it is a completely wireless experience! The sounds you hear are of the water gently flowing, the cicadas chirruping and children laughing and playing. To either side, trees and garrigue rise up and enfold you in their majesty; exquisite blue and green dragonflies hover like tiny helicopters just inches above the water's surface and silver fish swim gracefully by. In our village of Lagrasse, as you swim gently along the Orbière river, the thousand year old tower of the abbey looms into view above the treetops, silhouetted by the perfect blue of a cloudless Mediterranean sky.

Ribaute bridge

All these swimming spots are different in aspect. At Ribaute, just a couple of kilometres north of us, little waterfalls cascade over smooth rocks to form small pools whilst further upriver a large expanse of water allows for a proper swim. We pitch our chairs and shade umbrellas under the trees here to use as a base and to eat our picnic. Further downriver, beyond the waterfalls, an old bridge makes a perfect launch pad where the older French children jump 30 feet into the water, showing off in front of the flabbergasted visitors.

Ribaute

At La Bastide, another local village, water and time have conspired to carve a perfectly circular hole some ten feet below the rocks from where you can jump off. If you follow the narrow stretch of river up the gorge, you wade through little pools and waterfalls nestled amongst greenery and rock either side of you, until you reach a much larger pool with several jumping off places at least twenty feet in the air – perfect for the more intrepid teenagers.

Near the tiny village of Taurize, after negotiating a two kilometre long dirt track, a beautiful vista of lake and trees opens up, inviting you to spend the day mucking about in the water and even rowing around the lake if you're daft enough to have bought a massive three-man dinghy called "The Seahawk" like I did. The kids just love rowing out to the middle of the lake, pushing each other off and then not letting anyone get back on again.

Saint Laurent de la Cabrerisse

One of the most enchanting swimming spots is to be found near the village of Saint Laurent de la Cabrerisse. Here the flat-stone bed of the river steps down like a concertina so that the water flows on many levels allowing you to swim, dive off the rocks and even sit under miniature waterfalls that shower you in warm water. The setting is absolutely idyllic with a high rock face on one side and trees on the other. As with many of these swimming places, there are stone picnic tables here and there, with even a stone-built barbeque for you to use. The French think of everything.

Saint Laurent de la Cabrerisse

Although most days we choose the cheaper option of taking a picnic or barbeque to the places we visit, the alternative option of eating lunch at a restaurant near the swimming spot or beach is not to be missed. Obviously with a large family like ours it can prove to be expensive but with experience we have learned where to go and what to choose on the menus so as to allow us to take this option as often as we wish.

For instance, a favourite outing of ours is to drive through the Minervois, which is the region just north of the Corbières, to the breathtakingly beautiful village of Roquebrun situated inside the National Park of the Haut Languedoc.

Roquebrun

Most of the village is between 200 and 350 metres above sea level and more than 100 metres above the river Orb which flows from the mountains to the west. It is sheltered by hills to the north, east and west and boasts a microclimate in which oranges, lemons, pomegranates and palm trees flourish. In front of the village houses that pepper the sides of the hills stands a huge stone bridge which spans the river and it is under this that we bathe in the afternoon having indulged in bucket loads of (very reasonably priced) 'moules frites' at one of the charming hilltop restaurants. The chef confessed to me one day that the secret of why they are so good is that he buys them from Spain. For him, that still counted as local fare as the village is "only" three hours from the Spanish border.

Roquebrun

GASTRONOMY

There is an incredible variety of different restaurants in the region, from countryside auberges to city bistros and everything in between, but one specific type of cuisine stands out a mile. With a coastline stretching from Espiguette in the Camargue to Banyuls-sur-mer near the frontier with Spain, it's no surprise that there are plenty of great seafood restaurants to choose from. My favourites are the ones to be found in the same towns and villages where the oysters themselves are farmed. The oyster bays of Bouzigues and Leucate, part of the coast's "conchyliculture" (shellfish, oysters and mussels farming, to you!), produce the most fantastic oysters and naturally there are many restaurants here serving the freshest produce. A word of warning though: just because France has the very best restaurants in the world doesn't mean they are all good. A restaurant is only as good as the people who own, manage and work in it.

Bouzigues

The best restaurant for oysters and fresh fish that we have found so far is called "Le Petit Bouzigues". Small and unprepossessing on the outside, with amazing views of the oyster beds reaching out as far as the eye can see across the étang in front of the restaurant, its owner (and chef) knows exactly which seafood to serve and precisely how to prepare it. He chooses to serve "categorie 3" size oysters (actually just medium sized and the most common) because other sizes can be too "volumineux". His "plat du jour" on one of the days we visited was a simple sea bream but he had chosen to grill it with butter, garlic and herbs: absolutely delicious when chased down by the local wine "Picpoul de Pinet", a sharper white wine than most, produced in the next village along. Exquisite.

For the diehard seafood aficionado, there are rough and ready seafood bars in Leucate where the fishermen haul their catch in on one side of the shack, process the oysters, mussels, bulots (whelks), coquilles (scallops) and palourdes (clams) in the middle of the shack and then serve it all up on ice in the seating area. You get to watch them do all this while you wait. Don't overdress for the occasion as the floor can get pretty wet!

Superb view from the seafood buffet restaurant in Marseillan

Another seafood restaurant which stands out from the crowd is La Ferme Marine in Marseillan (not to be confused with Marseilles on the Cote d'Azur). On one of our weekends away, I had taken pot luck and reserved a table by calling a phone number on the internet but having no idea what to expect. For some reason it seems I am blessed with an almost supernatural 'Spidey-sense' when it comes to unearthing great restaurants (no idea why) and once again, I'm happy to say, my gastronomic ESP came good. Situated a short distance outside of Marseillan's main harbour, La Ferme Marine sits on the banks of the Étang with its oyster beds stretching out for miles into the distance.

Seafood heaven

Upon entering we were greeted by an incredible sight: mountains of ice piled upon a huge table bearing countless silver platters crammed with super-fresh oysters, sea snails, clams, whelks and the best prawns we have ever tasted. It was an all-you-can-eat buffet costing just €29.50 per person. With not a tourist in sight, the restaurant was packed to the gills with local French people and, ordering our favourite white wine (Picpoul de Pinet – 'black label'), we sat ourselves down and cheerfully joined in. Needless to say we did indeed consume all-we-could-eat.

Not content with infinite platefuls of seafood, Josef stuffs his pocket full of mussels just in case

I have returned many times to this superb restaurant since that first visit, often accompanied by my motley crew of friends. We all agree it is by far the best way to enjoy a lazy Sunday afternoon.

The village of Gruissan is a fishing port with a small harbour which now serves as a popular holiday destination for many French tourists. The old town in the centre is a delightful place for a stroll with its pleasant cafés and restaurants that pepper the narrow streets which surround the remains of an old castle, now known as Le Tour Barberousse ('Redbeard's Tower'). Originally built in the 10th century to guard against seaborne invaders and built on a steep, rocky hill, the castle was enlarged in the 12th century by the Archbishops of Narbonne, then dismantled in the 16th century on the orders of Cardinal Richelieu and left neglected ever since. Its stones were used to construct the village that encircles it.

Gruissan

La Cambuse du Saunier in Gruissan is a most unusual restaurant. Coupled with the boutique next door, it operates as the retail outlet for 'Le salin de Gruissan' or salt farm (aka 'saltern') of Gruissan. Located right at the edge of the salt plains, the restaurant affords you an exceptional view which changes colour during the day.

Salt mountains at Saint Martin

The salt plains will start off in the morning as a delicate blush of pastel colour and gradually, as the day goes on, 350 hectares of sodium chloride turn bright salmon pink. The pigment comes from salt-tolerant algae (dunaliella salina) whose colour intensifies as the local wind (the Cers) and the heat from the sun concentrate the salt solution. To one side a miniature salt mountain stands like a shimmering white mirage. We were reliably informed that the salt from Saint Martin's saltern is the result of a manufacturing technique that dates back to antiquity and we should of course take the owners at their word.

We were offered delicious oven roasted fish and meat marinated in the natural coarse salt, cuttlefish cassoulet, pan-seared shell-fish and a choice of Cassanova, Saint Martin or Fleur de Sel oysters, all climaxing with a 'fleur de sel' ice cream to finish off our meal. 'La fleur de sel' is formed when, during the summer at dawn, as the Cers wind blows, a fine layer of salt forms over the salt plains. Oddly, all this salt on the food gives each dish a subtle and savoury taste rather than overpowering you with salt, and serves to bring out the flavour of the dish. The local white wine from Gruissan - a very fresh Chardonnay – is inexpensive and complements the meal perfectly.

La Cambuse du Saunier

The Saltern's boutique next door, open 7 days a week, is fabulous. Stocked with every conceivable salt-based product – table salts (including the famous Fleur de Sel from Gruissan), natural and aroma-infused salts; 'Elixsels' or liquid salt; bath and body salts, natural salt crystals and coarse salt infused with spices – which make for brilliant and unusual gifts to take back to England. There's even an 'Eco-museum' attached to the boutique for those more intrepid explorers who would like to learn more about the history of sea salt production methods, with an exhibition of old tools used in the saltern, as well as information about Saint Martin's flora and fauna.

View from La Cambuse du Saunier restaurant

For that authentic holiday ambience, there is nothing more satisfying than dining on a star-filled night at one of the beach bar restaurants along the picturesque coast of the Mediterranean. Our favourites include Le Pilotis, Le Biquet, Le ZaZa bar and La Cote Rêvée (literally 'the dreamed-of coast'). All of these are either in or near Leucate where our favourite beaches are to be found; miles and miles of light, golden sands stretch out along the Mediterranean with stunning views of the snow-capped Pyrenees to the south which are sometimes shrouded in mist or cloud, at other times shimmering in the heat haze or just crystal clear in the distance. Another fantastic beach bar restaurant is La Voile Blanche ('the white sail') at Les Ayguardes in Gruissan, itself a delightful medieval seaside town complete with charming squares reached through narrow, cobbled streets. La Voile Blanche serves huge seafood or meat kebabs on skewers that defy description – you'll just have to go and try them yourself to find out.

Leucate beach – view from the bar

Don't worry – we went back and dug her up the following morning!

We are very fortunate to live close to one of France's three Michelin starred restaurants: L'Auberge du Vieux Puits in Fontjoncouse. It was awarded the honour in 2010 and how long it will remain a three Michelin starred restaurant is something only Michelin can answer but for now it is the pride of the Corbières gastronomy scene. The cuisine focuses on local foods, featuring simple ingredients such as cabbages, tomatoes and seasonal vegetables, lamb, goat, seasonal game (boar, hare, quail, and woodcock), pork from the Bigorre black pig, pigeon, picholine olives, rosemary, basil, cod, apples, potatoes (for example the Pays de Sault variety) and figs. Here, renowned chef Gilles Goujon and his staff create more a piece of theatre than a meal. If he serves prawns he will concoct an elaborate edible lattice to surround it; if he serves pigeon it may be encrusted in almond. A single poached oyster in sea water jelly is served with a huge, spherical pearl made of blown sugar and, once the thin film of the pearl is broken (a small mallet is provided for this purpose), beech wood smoke escapes and fills the nostrils with its delicate aroma. His signature dish, and the one most loved by his regular clientele, is called "L'oeuf pourri à la truffe" (rotten egg with truffles). Presented on a plate surrounded by a nest of straw, the poached egg is presented to you on a bed of mushrooms. At that point, the waiter will ceremoniously break the egg open in front of you, allowing a creamy sabayon of black truffle (with which the chef has replaced the original egg yolk) to flow out all over the egg white. Best rotten egg I've ever tasted!

L'Auberge du Vieux Puits dessert

Naturally, there is an incredible choice of local wines to savour, all lovingly itemised in an enormous, weighty wine menu that looks like a bible made of wood, and the service is as you would expect in a Michelin starred restaurant – without fault. When the meal is over, my advice is to just sign the cheque without looking at how much it all costs.

There are plenty of simpler, much cheaper alternatives in the area to choose from. The little café in Servies-en-val offers home cooked pizzas either with a base of creme fraiche or tomato in the square, opposite the village's lovely old chateau, where we have enjoyed evenings with friends and their children seated round extra-long tables. Another favourite pizzeria "Au Feu du Bois" is to be found in the small village of Talairan, with its pretty streets and church. This is a family run restaurant where all their ingredients are fresh and cooked in a wood-fired oven built into the wall. While we're on the subject of pizzas, you should not miss the opportunity to visit to Gus and Eva's place in Fabrezan called "L'Heureux Tour". Best pizzas outside Italy.

Inland, the Corbières has miles and miles of wild gorges with steep rocky walls, covered in trees and garrigue, through which streams and rivers run freely. The restaurants in the small villages here often have terraces where you can eat whilst enjoying these spectacular views. Our favourite is "Les Terrasses de la Berre" in Portel-des-Corbières which is best enjoyed in the evening as the sun sets over the gorge and surrounding hills. Definitely not for people with a fear of heights.

A final mention has to go to the Calicots restaurant in nearby village of Fabrezan. Hidden away in a warren of cobbled streets, the Calicots is home to one of our favourite local delicacies – 'mussels in aniseed'.

Les Terrasses de la Berre restaurant in Portel-des-Corbières

**Our daughters Grace and Lucy at the
Calicots restaurant in Fabrezan**

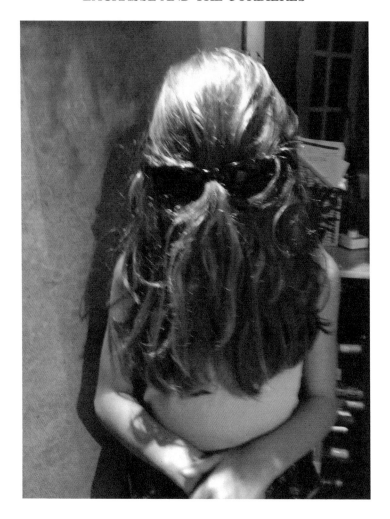

**What happens after eating the 'mussels in aniseed'
at Calicots restaurant!**

EN ROUTE

The American poet Ralph Waldo Emerson famously once said 'Life is a journey, not a destination' and, with this in mind, allow me to offer you a brief account of the diverse ways of travelling from England to this wonderful region of France.

Any helpers?!

The Occitanie is a thousand miles from our English home and so flying with Ryanair on one of its affordable flights to Carcassonne, Beziers, Montpellier, Toulouse, Perpignan or even to Gerona just over the border in Spain, is the quickest and most convenient method.

On arrival at the airport in France, a car is essential in order to explore this vast region. We hire an inexpensive little run-around when we go for long weekends but during the summer holidays we rent a 7-seater for our ever growing family. This option is expensive however and so recently, for the first time, we chose to drive from England in our own MPV.

With four children in tow it is definitely advisable to stopover for a night – the drive from our home in England is an exhausting sixteen hours in total – and so we chose Chartres, with its enormous cathedral and myriad restaurants as our regular overnight stop.

Chartres Cathedral

It takes eight hours to drive to Chartres from our home in England and then eight hours to reach the French house the following day. We chose to stay at the ever reliable IBIS hotel in the centre of Chartres (although we've since switched to the Mercure which is better still) and once we'd had a little nap and freshened up after the first leg of our journey, we set off on foot for the old town centre huddled in the shadow of its famous cathedral. After our meal (at an excellent Crêperie in the main street) we retraced our steps and enjoyed the amazing light show that is projected over a hundred metres all the way up the flamboyant cathedral's facade to the accompaniment of tasteful atmospheric music and warm applause from the enthusiastic crowds. These kind of "son-et-lumière" extravaganzas are what the French are so rightly famous for. What a great way to spend the evening of a stopover.

'Trompe l'oeil' painted onto building in Chartres

One of the main reasons for buying a house in France was that, as a large family, we were getting fed up with paying extortionate prices for renting a villa with a pool somewhere in Europe each summer. Now we have much cheaper accommodation costs (the French versions of English council tax – taxe foncière and taxe d'habitation – come to around €1000 a year) and we can stay as long as we like. In addition, as a manufacturers' agent helping companies to export their goods within mainland Europe, I use the house as a base for visiting both customers and suppliers. Each year in spring and autumn I travel down to our French house in my comfortable old Mercedes for a few months at a time and, with the assistance of a Wi-Fi router, laptop, an all-in-one printer/copier/scanner and a telephone, I work out of an office on the top floor of our village house. From there I take the opportunity to visit customers in Belgium, Holland, Germany, Switzerland and France. From my 'French office', I have even driven all the way to Italy, where my Principals' factories are located, travelling through Provence and the Cote d'Azur. You can't beat stopping in Fréjus for a spot of lunch en route and eating alfresco in full sun with a glorious view of the Mediterranean Sea.

Hotel Les Deux Chèvres

On the trip down from England, I often stay at the same hotel in Burgundy for a stopover. Les Deux Chèvres is an excellent family-owned hotel in the cosy village of Gevrey-Chambertin, home to some of the very best Burgundy wines and I always try to stock up my modest wine collection with a case or two of the fabulous vintages to be had in the region. Somewhat unusually, the hotel is owned by a Welshman and his Polish wife; Paul and Yolante are the best hosts and always make you feel so very welcome. They have renovated a large, old village house that boasts a courtyard and a terrace at the rear with unobstructed views to the vineyards beyond. The rooms are incredible; my favourite is off the courtyard and was once the old kitchen of the house with its huge stone fireplace and bread ovens set into the walls. I love the mix of old world charm with modern conveniences: the shower (or wet-room) is state-of-the-art and the mattress and linen have been carefully chosen to ensure a blissfully peaceful night's sleep.

Bedroom at Les Deux Chèvres

Courtyard bedroom at Les Deux Chèvres

No wonder the hotel was recently voted number one in Burgandy on TripAdvisor. In the evening, I enjoy tucking into pre-dinner amuse-bouches of the host's home-made "escargots en croute" accompanied by a "coup de champagne" before sauntering out for dinner at Chez Guy, the restaurant in the heart of the village, and treating myself to an expensive bottle of the local vintage. Simply unmissable. Check out the hotel's website and treat yourselves – www.lesdeuxchevres.com.

The motorways in France are an absolute dream. I wish the authorities in England would consider investing in more toll roads; the enjoyment of one's journey is vastly enhanced by the lack of traffic and the superior quality of road surface. To enhance the experience further, I recently purchased one of those electronic tags for the car that allow for an uninterrupted drive through the numerous "Péages" without stopping to collect or pay for a ticket. You are simply invoiced each month by Sanef Tolling which makes the journey so much quicker and easier. No more getting out of the car to take a ticket or to pay which used to guarantee annoying the hell out of the left-hand drive French car's owner behind.

Finally, on the approach to Lagrasse itself, there are several ways to arrive but the most direct route (especially from the airport in Carcassonne, just 35 minutes away by car) is to take the road through the villages of Fabrezan and Ribaute which snakes its way through the countryside with impressive views of the river and gorges below and the Alaric mountains beyond, until rounding a final bend on the crest of a hill where, from this high vantage point, Lagrasse reveals itself in all its splendour. Nestled in the hills of the Corbières, with far-reaching views all the way to the Pyrenees in the south, the village appears like a jewel set in the emerald green of the garrigue under a sapphire-blue sky, where the Orbière river meanders nonchalantly under two old stone, vaulted bridges and flows alongside the Benedictine abbey that blesses the whole with its munificence.

Lagrasse – Jewel of the Corbières

VILLAGE LIFE

View from the riverside café Le Recantou in Lagrasse

It goes without saying that I owe a great deal of my inspiration for writing this kind of book to Peter Mayle's best seller "A Year in Provence". Since he published his celebrated work back in 1989 there has been a plethora of similarly themed offerings covering subjects such as living in France, buying a house in France, olive growing in France, making wine in France and so on and so on. However, if you are like me, you will nevertheless happily purchase a newly-published book/travelogue at the airport before your holiday because, whilst these kinds of books all have the country of

France in common, everyone's experience is different and the authors' circumstances vary drastically, offering the reader a fresh perspective on the subject every time. I hope this book proves to be no exception.

In Peter Mayle's book, having bought a run-down farmhouse in Provence, he gives a humorous account of the characters he encounters; a hotchpotch of comical yet endearing French tradesmen. I'm not sure I can offer the same here, as all the characters in our village are pretty much sane. What's more, Lagrasse is different in that it boasts a large percentage of residential expats, unlike Mayle's nearby villages of Bonnieux and Ménerbes back in the Eighties when foreigners buying second homes in France was a relatively new phenomenon. The local French population in Lagrasse are either down-to-earth "Midi" people who tend the vines, or, as stonemasons and labourers, help rebuild the old village houses; others form part of the tourist industry running restaurants, cafés, art galleries, manning the tourist office and the Heritage Museum (La Maison du Patrimoine). Some of the French inhabitants have retired here or settled, like the expats, to indulge in the many cultural advantages of living in a historic, medieval village and generally just to relax and soak up the friendly, laidback atmosphere of the place with its deserved reputation for the arts, crafts and literature.

Many of the cultural events that take place in Lagrasse are held inside, or in the grounds of, the remarkable 8th century Benedictine abbey, Sainte-Marie d'Orbieu. It is the largest abbey in the Aude region and is classed as a historical monument. It was commissioned by Charlemagne, who, when he first came to the village, commented on the underdeveloped fields and countryside, with its paucity of foodstuffs and agricultural land, and charismatically decided, from then on, to make the area more fertile and productive, which gave the village its name 'Lagrasse', meaning the fat or fertile place.

Three times a year – spring, summer and autumn – the abbey plays host to the "Banquet du Livre", one of France's most respected literature, poetry and philosophy festivals. Writers and philosophers from all over the world are invited to attend and lecture on their specialist subjects. Other events held here, sometimes outside in the grounds, have included plays, classical music concerts and modern circus acts; one year, it even hosted a performance by dancers from the Royal Ballet. The magical setting of the old abbey makes occasions like these very special for anyone who is fortunate enough to be present.

Lagrasse abbey Sainte-Marie d'Orbieu

The abbey's buildings are arranged round a small courtyard with its two wooden galleries supported by Romanesque columns. There's an abbot's dwelling, a wonderful chapel whose walls still bear traces of paintings of the Tree of Life and the Last Judgement; a former sacristy and transept; a ceremonial hall, various rooms with huge fireplaces and barrel-vaulted ceilings; a gatehouse, a storeroom and bake-house, and, for use by the present occupants, an infirmary and enormous dormitory. Some of the floors are paved with priceless enamelled terracotta tiles dating from the 14th century. The oldest part of the abbey, including the 40 metres high bell tower, is owned by the Aude authorities. However, the part that was completed in later centuries is presently occupied by a religious community of Augustine monks who call themselves the "Chanoines Réguliers de la Mère de Dieu". The monks can sometimes be seen in their flowing robes, walking the hills, deep in contemplation and, just occasionally, jogging in the hills!

In contrast, the superbly irreligious festival of the ABRACADAGRASSES is held in July under the awnings of the Market Hall, and peppered around the village's bars and cafés. Musicians and bands come from all over the world and do their funky thing for three days and nights. We get everything from brass disco-punk, Mandingo blues, Reggae roots and Electronic folk to Tropical Dance Floor Bass Music, Afro-psychedelic, Folk Cajun, psychedelic spirit of Peruvian cumbia...I could go on. The bands have great names like The Dizzy Brains and the Sax Peace Tools. Just think Glastonbury without the mud.

As I have already mentioned, there is a high percentage of expats and artists living in the village. I should apologise in advance if you think I'm clearly overly impressed by the background and accomplishments of my fellow villagers, but for a provincial lad from the shires to be given the chance to mix with such interesting

Abracadagrasses concert.

Grand Guignol puppets at the Abracadagrasses festival

people, has been a rare privilege. At one time or another, Lagrasse has been home to the wife of the heir to an English Dukedom, who chose to get married here at the abbey, concluding the ceremony with a ride through the streets on an authentic golden carriage that once belonged to an English monarch; an erstwhile principal dancer of the Royal Ballet; many painters, potters, sculptors, writers and talented musicians; historians, photographers, newspaper editors; artisans such as upholsterers, ébénistes, menuisiers, dress designers and, to cap it all, no less than three Oxford and Cambridge dons.

Josef expounds on his theory of everything to lobster-less Kev

Probably the most well-loved member of the English expat brigade is "Josef the Artist" as he is affectionately known. Joe is one of the reasons we decided to take the plunge and buy a house here. When we were holidaying in the village the year before we bought the house, we stayed in the gite next-door to Joe's painting studio and throughout our stay, Josef made our whole family feel so welcome. He has a totally engaging and disarming charm; the children all fell in love with him. He is rarely to be seen without a kaleidoscopically paint-splattered artist's smock draped haphazardly over his shoulders and a glass of rosé in his hand. If you're really lucky he will have positioned a small table and chairs outside the door to his gallery and will never fail to ask you to join him in a libation (or what Joe sometimes refers to as a pan-galactic gargle blaster). The expats call this experience "Joe's bar".

We have several of Josef's paintings in our house (my initial resolution when we first bought the house was to try to adorn it solely with art from local artisans). To that effect we have Joe's paintings, a Henry Blackmore (more about Henry later), Annie's colourful pottery (Annie is a sweet French lady with a shop/outlet on the Promenade whose pottery, often somewhat disturbingly, comprises spooky eyes, snakes and insects) and Shona's amazing river pebble lamps. The small flat pebbles, which can be white, grey, brown or even painted red, black and other colours, are sourced from the local rivers and are then carefully glued together to form a circular shape; at night they cast an explosion of light onto the nearby surfaces, walls and ceilings, creating a warm, intimate effect.

Shona is also the first port of call for anyone wanting to rent a room or gite in the village. Previously an estate agent, she now runs a Chambre d'Hote at her home "Chez Shona" in Rue Magene and lets out local houses as gites for families or even larger bookings. Her website address is www.stay-in-lagrasse.com and she comes highly recommended.

One of Shona's amazing pebble lamps

Shona's studio

As I have already explained, the covered market hall in the main square (Place de la Halle) is surrounded on all sides by some of the very best houses in the village dating from the 14th and 15th centuries often with wrought iron balconies and boasting large sun terraces at the rear facing the river Orbière. Some of these houses are let as gites by our friends. Kate and Roger (www.holidayslagra sse .com) let three separate apartments within the same house and Nicole (www.houselafrance.com) lets two more. Roger has just returned from backpacking in the Far East and is no stranger to travel: he once organised a three month canoe trip up an unexplored tributary of the Amazon. An accomplished guitarist, he plays in the local festivals with his jazz/rock fusion band 'Small Talk' and has also recently set up 'Locations Vélos' from one of the downstairs rooms that gives onto the square, renting bicycles to the tourists. When Kate is not riding a horse from Land's End to John O'Groats, she is often to be found riding through the vineyards and the Corbières hills. Nicole's house next-door is absolutely beautiful; painted white throughout with long flowing chiffon lace curtains swelling in the breeze, a huge open kitchen and what must be the largest terrace in the village with wonderful views of the river, abbey and hills beyond. Other good friends of ours, Claire and Guy, originally from Cornwall, let four apartments/studios nearby from a beautiful house that features a garden and swimming pool. Years ago, after buying the house, Guy's monumental renovation work revealed more than he was bargaining for. Here's an excerpt from their website (www.holidaysinlagrasse.com):

"Guy bought the house in 2004 and after a 5 year and 600-ton renovation, he uncovered the secrets of the property providing some of the most amazing architecture, sculptures and paintings from the Cathar period. The historic paintings where found by chance. To the naked eye they were old planks on a ceiling but hidden by what we now know as layers of fly poo! If it had not rained on the scattered boards in the garden overnight, Guy would never have seen the colours revealed. In total, there are 128 planks, with the longest measuring 4.8m. Guy stored them for 7 years and on showing Claire, both agreed it was important for them to be preserved and shared with the community so contact was made with the Mairie. The boards are currently being renovated. To date, 26 have been cleaned and revealed fantasy animals, Fleur de Lis, 3 kings, one believed to be King John, also known as 'John with no lands' and 22 chevaliers, one of which is Simon de Montfort and a local family crest identifying the family Lévis who instructed the building of the great bell tower at Lagrasse Abbey. These paintings are believed to be the oldest paintings in the region and have caused great interest with medieval specialists across Europe. We continue to work with the Bâtiments de France to understand how the paintings are linked with the Cathar Crusade and how they elaborate on the story during the Cathar period." As discoveries go, I'd say that beats finding a coin down the back of the sofa.

Other great friends of ours are Barry and Hannah who have lived in the village for some time now and own a cool, hidden-away house on the bank of the river by the abbey. We have spent some very enjoyable, lazy afternoons with them there, enjoying barbecues and eating the cherries from their fruit tree. Barry is a well-known photographer and will regale you with tales of the rich and famous who have sat for him. If he isn't getting Terry Gilliam, the film director and Monty Python member, to pose for him hanging precariously from the balcony of one of his film sets while Barry sits back and giggles, he is taking photos of such luminaries as Fidel Castro, General Pinochet, Mick Jagger, Michael Moore, William Hague, Michael Palin, Donny "don't make me look camp" Osmond and Eartha Kitt, to name but a few. He is given his own tent at Glastonbury Festival every year by the owner, Michael Eavis, in return for photographing the festival goers and their goings-on, mainly in the notorious Naughty Corner on the outskirts of the main festival area, celebrated for its outsider art and underground culture. As I write, his new book – 'Vaguely Lost in Shangri-La' – has been published in 2017 to rave reviews and I heartily recommend that you purchase it and place it in your possession. You can buy it from the website: www.thefloodgallery.com. Dazzling dinner conversation always guaranteed if you're sat next to Barry.

A relatively new event, which takes place in July every year in the open space of the Market Hall, is the piano and classical music concert 'En Blanc et Noir' (www.enblancetnoir.com). Organised by English pianist, Robert and friends, they invite musicians from Music Conservatoires all over Europe (and sometimes beyond) to come and perform together over five days in the summer. The event is funded entirely from donations and admission is offered free of charge to everyone, which is a rare and wonderful thing. When the festival first began, the event manager promoting the concerts, and being the hostess with the most-est at the end of event party, was another friend, Beverley, a wonderfully vibrant personality who made everyone feel welcome and ensured the smooth running of the event. Beverley owns and runs a designer dress and hand-made jewellery shop in the village. She designs and makes the dresses herself. Check out her website: www.beverleysmart.com.

En Blanc et Noir

During the performances given by the musicians at 'En Blanc et Noir', people have been moved to tears by the inspired playing and charged atmosphere. I remember one Russian violinist, accompanied on piano by an Englishman, who after having tried his best to keep his sheet music pinned to the music stand for the opening number, whilst battling in vain against the infamously strong wind that can appear out of nowhere in our village, suddenly threw the music sheets to the wind and declared that it didn't matter because they would simply play all the pieces they knew by heart! This made for a much more personal and spirited rendition of the songs which held the audience in rapture and was naturally met by tumultuous applause.

In 2015, the expats mucked in together and arranged a V.E. day 70th anniversary celebration, which, like the classical music concert, also took place under the awnings of the Market Hall in the main square. The houses in the square were duly festooned with the national flags of the countries that took part in the war and, billowing in the wind, gave the setting its festive ambience.

The market square – VE day

Guests were invited to attend in traditional dress of the 1940's and many of the French locals donned white shirts, black waistcoats and berets whilst the ladies wore 1940's summer dresses and fancy hats. Guy, one of the local expats, won first prize for his take on an English airman complete with swirly moustache and a long white scarf that stuck straight out at 180 degrees thanks to the canny use of a bent, metal clothes hanger. Looked hilarious!

Guy and Claire play to the gallery!

Locals dished out an enormous pan of paella, including langoustines, and a chicken chasseur, whilst others volunteered to man the trestle-table bars that lined the square, offering wine and local artisan beer to all and sundry.

VE Day fare

The main organiser of the event, Sandra, had seconded a three-piece swing band into serenading us throughout the night; a perfect choice for the occasion. Not everything ran smoothly though. A few days before the event it was pointed out to Sandra (in *sotto voce* by some of the French locals) that German and Italian flags were conspicuous by their absence and perhaps the emphasis should really be on reconciliation after all? There ensued a mad scramble to find the errant standards and eventually the only flags that could be found were a tenth of the size of all the others! Hopefully no-one took offence though; there were certainly plenty of resident German nationals who attended the event and who heartily joined in with and contributed to the spirit of the evening.

Somewhat typically for Lagrasse, where you never really know what's going to happen next, a reincarnation of Mahatma Gandhi also made an appearance at the VE celebration! Leaving aside the fact that Gandhi himself was not amongst the many Indians who died fighting the Axis powers (he had of course refused to fight for the allies until India was made independent; he was banged up in prison from 1942 to 1945), the presence of the great pacifist was not unwelcome, just rather surprising. Arriving unannounced right in the middle of proceedings dressed in white Indian robes, shaven-headed and wielding the famous long walking stick, one of the local French guys proceeded to make his way slowly through the crowds to the stage and once there mumbled a few unintelligible words into the microphone, ending with a blessing of peace and love upon the whole gathering and departed to cheers of bemused gratitude from the audience. Apparently, I was told later, he does this sort of thing regularly. Utterly bizarre.

The final 'deal clincher' for me, when I was deciding whether to take the plunge and buy a house all those years ago, was meeting an old school friend unexpectedly at a party given by our mutual friends, Richard and Johanna, at their newly renovated house just off the market square. They had spent a good few years 'attacking' their 15th century house, installing new flooring, pointing interior walls, building bathrooms from scratch and so on and so forth, even having to endure cold showers outside in the alley whilst the work progressed; and had finally manhandled the house into a (much more than) presentable state so that they could throw a party. Richard was once a Principal Dancer for the Royal Ballet and, in his retirement, exhibited his photography in the village, a great deal of which was shot backstage at theatres visited during his long career with refreshingly informal stills of famous luminaries of the ballet world, such as Rudolf Nureyev. At the party I wandered into the kitchen in search of a refill and got talking to a tall, attractive lady (as you do) discussing the fine improvements that the house's owners had recently achieved, when the conversation turned to asking where we were both originally from in England. The lady said she was from Wolverhampton and I said "Oh that's funny, so am I". Then I said "Well, which school did you go to?" and she replied "Tettenhall College" and I said "Well so did I!" "But what year were you there?" said the mystery lady and we quickly realised that we must both have attended the school at the same time. By this point a small crowd of the other guests had gathered around us, no doubt drawn by the rising volume levels and excitement of the protagonists playing verbal ping pong, when suddenly the penny dropped and I blurted out in final recognition "Emma __!" and she shouted back "Stuart Benton!" The crowd of guests nearly applauded we had put on such a show. Actually we hadn't really changed that much over time: Emma's hair was a different colour and my once svelte figure had 'naturally' adjusted itself over time to accommodate all the good French cuisine I had indulged in to date but I suppose thirty years is a long time and who would have expected to meet an old friend a thousand miles from where you originally knew them? Anyway, after revisiting all the events of our school years, the best news was that, like me, Emma had married her childhood sweetheart whom she had met at our school and he was none other than my old mate Bill who I had also known and got on very well with. In seconds Emma was on the phone to him in London and I managed a short "Yes, it's really me!" conversation with him and he promised to look us up as soon as he was back in France. We have remained in contact ever since and now see them both every year. It's a small world.

Emma and Bill, with their daughter Amelie, had bought an interesting property some years ago just a few kilometres from Lagrasse. The house, which is called Les Quatre Vents (The Four Winds) due to its elevated position, is rented out (whenever Emma and Bill aren't in residence) to large families of sun lovers in the spring and summer or more recently to parties of wild boar hunters in the autumn/winter season who come for the authentic experience. Perched on a hilltop and set in 20 hectares of pine forest, the large house had originally been designed and built by a Belgian architect and when I first visited the house my initial impression was that it reminded me of the kind of house J.G. Ballard would conjure up for his science fiction stories, such was its unusual and futuristic appearance.

Les Quatre Vents

Although it was a one story building from the outside, the entire first floor had been replicated underground. The main room on the first floor was a huge open plan lounge, dining room and kitchen area with large French doors (what else?) leading to a terrace with magnificent views of the surrounding land and an enormous stone barbecue around which a party-size table and chairs were set.

Emma describes the story behind the initial purchase on her website:

"We were on holiday in the Corbières and chanced upon Les Quatre Vents by accident. It was love at first sight. The views, space and tranquil atmosphere literally blew us away. However, vision goggles were required because the house was in disrepair and the forest was totally over-grown. So, we came back from holiday with a house. As my mother said, "most people come back with a few bottles of wine but you..." Anyway, it is a labour of love as we gradually restore the estate. It is a place where you can think and truly relax. A great antidote to our busy lives."

It was here that my family enjoyed our first meal with Bill and Emma. Em had bought a huge leg of lamb from the local farmer which she duly garnished with garlic and herbs from the garrigue. It was in the process of being cooked on the barbecue when we arrived and, once our glasses were filled to the brim with a regional wine that Bill knew we'd enjoy, we all sat outside and relaxed. Accompanied by a starter of fresh bread and baked camembert stuffed with more herbs and garlic, the meal was one of those unforgettable "French" meals that our children and their parents will remember for years to come. Seated outside, enveloped by the warm air and the heady scent of lavender, thyme and rosemary emanating from the surrounding landscape, accompanied by the sounds of amorous frogs and the cicadas, we talked and laughed and drank the night away. During the evening, Emma related a memorable anecdote of how, at a birthday party at Les Quatre Vents, she'd been approached by one of the guests who, unbeknown to Emma was supposedly 'psychic' and was told that, in the distant past, Emma had in fact been a beautiful Cathar Princess, that Bill had been her warrior guardian and that unfortunately the psychic lady had, at the time, been the one who'd had to kill her! Not to be put off, Emma is now more than happy to believe every word, has no time for sceptics and insists the story must be completely true. Well, who can blame her?

Earlier on, Bill was explaining to me about how he spent the days shimmying up the trees that had grown so tall as to have blocked out the light and the view, cutting them down to size with a chainsaw, and how much he enjoyed doing that compared with the day job back in England. At one point he took me aside and, pointing to a faraway, dusky purple line in the distance that I had to squint to see, informed me that this was the river which demarcated the boundary of his land!

On the way back to our village later that night I had to make sure I didn't drive into any wild boar that were known to dart out onto the road in the dark; luckily for all involved we didn't meet any. As it happens, the next time I was invited to Bill and Emma's house, I would be ceremoniously offered one on a plate.

In order to maximise the rental potential of Les Quatre Vents, Emma had come up with the idea of inviting parties of hunters to holiday at the house during the autumn and winter months. I was duly invited with our mutual friend David, who also lives in our village, to come for a photo shoot posing as rough and ready hunter types and have our pictures taken feasting on wild boar around the dining table. Well, David and I are really the last people on earth to be able to convincingly masquerade as blood-thirsty killers and even though we tried our best to look the part, waving huge chunks of boar meat through the air on the ends of hunting knives whilst quaffing copious goblets of red wine, the overall effect was more like a couple of poets on the piss enjoying a boozy lunch! Understandably due to our inability to carry off the desired Asterix and Obelisk effect, Emma decided quite rightly not to use the photos in the final publicity material. Oh well, at least David and I can vouch for the fact that there really is such a thing as a free lunch.

The grounds of Les Quatre Vents boast a huge swimming pool (22 x 7 metres) adjacent to a contemporary summer kitchen and dining area (designed and built by David) and a tennis court guaranteeing a great time for all the guests lucky enough to holiday here. Feel free to visit their website: www.les4vents.com. Obviously, we are looking forward to spending lots more time with Emma and Bill.

Our other favourite Francophiles are the wonderful Tom and

Sarah. We were first introduced to them by Bill and Emma when we all met for a slap-up meal for fourteen people at La Fargo, a restaurant near the village of Saint Pierre, where we sat outside one balmy evening enjoying the beautiful setting and excellent company. As I've already stated, it's been great fun and a real eye-opener to meet so many people in the Occitanie heralding from so many different parts of the globe and with such diverse backgrounds and life stories, and Tom and Sarah are no exception. Tom attended Harrow school and we were eventually to be introduced to more old Harrovians and the odd Etonian (excuse the 'odd' Jim!) which offered us an insight into a world we'd never encountered before. Are you the same as me? Do you labour under the misconception that most people fortunate enough to have attended these top-drawer schools are often aloof and stand-offish? Perhaps one or two famous politicians spring to mind? Well, fortunately, I can now vouch for the fact that this certainly doesn't apply to every former pupil. Tom and his friends are all down-to-earth, exceptionally friendly and great fun to be around. Tom's a fantastic father to his children and the best company. Our families have spent countless hours together almost always involving water to some degree (oh yes and some alcohol too). Tom's wife, Sarah, is a super-intelligent lady and she and I hit it off from the word go with our shared love of all things French (well most things French) as well as art, literature and the classical world. They have three children: Emma, Milly and Bea, who are roughly the same ages as our children and so it was obviously ideal for us to meet up when holidaying 'en famille' in the Aude. Besides the many trips to the beaches and river swimming spots together, we often find time to visit the 'Lac de la Cavayère' which is Carcassonne's lake. Here we treat our families to long afternoons bouncing the life out of a dozen huge inflatables.

Inflatable children and their Mums

Inflatable heaven

Inflatable merry-go-round

If we're really lucky we are invited to lunch or dinner 'al fresco' at Sarah's mother's house in Pradelles-en-val, a little village near Lagrasse. After negotiating what must be the longest and bumpiest driveway in France, upon arrival you are treated to the most fantastic views of the valleys ('vals') stretching out for miles with the hills in the distance. Patsy and little Noisette (Sarah's Mum and her dog) greet you at the old farmhouse and beckon you round the side of its pretty garden to the typically French, extra-long table which is sometimes, if you're really lucky, set with fresh asparagus, salad and marinated prawns under the large, old mulberry tree whose leaves offer you the most welcome shade from the hot sun, while the kids all run off to the heavenly swimming pool down the path a little way.

**Patsy's infinitely lovely swimming pool
and view in Pradelles-en-val**

To return to my discourse on life in our village, it is quite unusual in rural France to have a bar that stays open late at night but fortunately for us, Lucy and her wife Sandrine run the "Coupa" on the Promenade which expats and locals alike use as the "pub" in the evening. Here they sell local wine and beer as well as ice cream, steak haché burgers and paninis (our kids' favourite). Lucy's a real occitan girl and if you can understand her strong midi accent you can understand any French person. Both girls are warm-hearted, friendly and always cheerful, making sure everyone has fun late into the night. Their favourite French band is 'Telephone', whom I remember fondly from my teenage years spent in France, and whose music Lucy often blasts out from her ghetto blaster during the evenings to liven up the experience. The girls also put on live bands of gypsy musicians who play wild renditions of folk songs on acoustic guitars and violins, and sometimes reggae bands (Biggz General, a grandson of Bob Marley, played here one night with his band). Many evenings have been spent supping at the Coupa interspersed with long hours of pétanque (French boules) opposite the bar on the purpose-built gravel courtyard under the plane trees. Pétanque is an ideal sport to play in France because of the warm weather and it is not uncommon for "parties" of boules to be played out into the small hours – in fact the locals seem to play better the more wine they drink. My good friend Xavier, a white-skinned Rastafarian complete with dreadlocks down to his waist, hosts the pétanque competition every Friday night with bottles of (just about palatable) wine for the winners and "merde alors" for the losers. I got so into my pétanque that I eventually went the whole hog and popped along to the sports shop in nearby Lezignan to have some boules made specially for me. They take the size of your throwing hand, ask you the weight you'd like and the design, then make you bespoke ones. Only trouble is I can't live without them now! Along with my neighbour and good friend, Henry, a fellow Englishman, together we make up 'The Boules Brothers' and, much to the chagrin of the locals, have won several finals and lots of bottles of wine. Allez les Blancs!

Pétanque

Henry lives next door with his brother Will, whose ever-so-French girlfriend Estelle works as a waitress at the fabulous village restaurant on the Promenade called La Cocotte Felée (The Cracked Pot). This restaurant is owned and run by its two chefs, Guillaume and Gregoire, who used to work at another restaurant in the village called Le Temps des Courges (literally 'courgette time' but colloquially means something like 'time for the nutters'). Guillaume and Greg have travelled a great deal in Asia/Indochina and consequently wanted to open a local restaurant serving a fusion of Asian and French cuisine; French tradition with an Asian twist – totally addictive. Greg's large family (he has five siblings in all) are the local olive growers "Les Oliviers" and you have not lived until you have enjoyed a tub of their garlic/herb olives for sale from Lagrasse's renowned Saturday market. The market takes place every Saturday morning in the Place de la Halle under the eaves of the Market Hall and attracts tourists and villagers alike. The stalls are run by local artisans and sell, amongst other things, jewellery, paintings, olives, fruit and veg, honey, goats' cheese (sold by a guy who looks an awful lot like God with his long white hair and flowing white beard), artisanal beer and, more recently, Thai food which is delicious.

Produce at the local market

My Boules Brother and I were often joined on the pétanque court by the Irish artist, painter, sculptor and raconteur Henry Blackmore and his wonderful wife Sheila who have been my great friends since they upped sticks some years ago, leaving their four grown-up daughters to fend for themselves back in Dublin, and moved to France as full-time residents. Sadly, Henry passed away in 2017. He was a dear friend and is greatly missed by all who knew him. Henry created the most amazing paintings in a magic-realism style with a strong Irish folkloric influence. The paintings have great depth and multiple layers of meaning. If you take time to study and enjoy each painting, you will be rewarded by hidden images unexpectedly emerging from the canvas; ones you would not have noticed if you had only given the paintings a cursory glance. Secreted figures, animals and faces, like that of the writer James Joyce, for instance, will gradually reveal themselves, adding

'Bloomsday' – Henry Blackmore

Henry and Sheila

new layers of meaning to his delightful works of art. Henry earned his crust selling his work or offering art courses for paying guests who wanted to learn to paint or just improve their skill at painting whilst enjoying a holiday in the south of France. His work is still exhibited in art galleries in Dublin as well as many of our local village restaurants. A visit to his website is most definitely recommended: www.henryblackmore.com.

As I'm here in the village on my lonesome working from the office for much of the year, my many friends and neighbours take pity on me and regularly invite me round for dinner, birthday parties and the like. These occasions are always memorable because everyone here without exception has a shared interest in great cuisine. Doris and Joerg are my next-door neighbours and, hailing as they do from Frankfurt in Germany, I am often treated to a banquet of the best of German gastronomy. From bratwurst and sauerkraut (who'd have thought fermented cabbage salad could taste so good!) washed down with copious amounts of wheat beer; to roulade and 'knoedel' (dumplings to you) finished off with good old-fashioned 'Schwarzwalder Kirschtorte', or Black Forest gateau (the cake is named after 'Schwarzwalder Kirschwasser' which is a liqueur distilled from tart cherries – so now you know).

Recently, for Joerg's birthday, Doris outdid herself with a meal that was a fusion of French and German dishes each accompanied by a different local French wine. She even typed out the menu for her guests with photos of the Corbières alongside to make us feel like we were dining in a Michelin starred restaurant. Hervé and Marie-Claude from over the road arrived bearing gifts of a bottle of wine and a ginormous leg of 'sanglier' (wild boar) which must have been nearly half a metre long. Before dinner, Hervé, true to form, treated us all to photos on his smartphone of the hairy, bloody corpses of the seven sangliers he had just that very morning dispatched with his gun much to the consternation of the German dinner guests.

As the only Englishman around the table, I felt somewhat outnumbered but fortunately I speak German as well as French so the conversation flowed as freely as the beer, wine and schnapps.

**Joerg bites off more than he can chew
with Hervé's gift of leg of sanglier**

The first course was a terrine of foie gras and langoustine (force-feeding geese until their livers expand to ten times their normal volume is not something I buy into but when in Rome...). Described as 'surf and turf' on the printed menu, we discovered in conversation that whilst the French also have their own term for it ('terre et mer'), the Germans don't. Doris said the closest Germany had got to a translation was 'fifty-fifty' which is just cheating because that's English of course. Next up was salmon and spinach 'en croute' in a tarragon sauce made with the local bubbly Crémant-de-Limoux which went down a treat, and the following cheese course included a French cheese with Greek fennel and a strong blue from the Pyrenees. Topped off with a pudding of figs in a red fruit jus, the meal had been a resounding success and everyone departed after many hugs and kisses and the sworn promise to start the diet the very next day.

(Vigne des Corbières en automne)

24 septembre 2016 – Dîner d'anniversaire de Jörg

Apéritif :
Champagne, Lucques, grissinis, duo de tomates cerise et concombres farcis

***

Terre et mer : terrine de foie gras à la langouste et chutney de mangue
Toques et clochers Autan

***

Feuilleté de saumon-épinards-farce d'églefin, sauce estragon
au Crémant de Limoux, riz de l'Aude
Lafage Cadireta

***

Plateau de fromage, petits pains maison
Château la Voulte- Gasparets

***
Duo de figues à la panna cotta caramélisée

***
Café, pousse-café

Amuses-Bouches chez Doris

**Hervé recounts another nail-biting,
bloodcurdling hunting story**

A PHOTOGRAPHIC TOUR
OF LAGRASSE

Abbey in winter

Aerial shot of Lagrasse

Place de la Halle

Misty Abbey

Lagrasse and abbey at night

Historic photo of the old abbey

Porte d'eau (14th century) – the last remaining gateway

Maison Maynard – Place de la Halle

**Maison Lautier – the house was built around 1530
- check out that door!**

Close-up of the old door at the side of Maison Lautier

The Promenade and its plane trees

Restaurant La Cocotte Felée

War memorial and 1900 museum

Lagrasse river before flooding

Lagrasse river after flooding

Lagrasse alleyway ("ruelle" in French)

The Occitan independence shield outside the village Epicerie
with its slogan meaning:
"We want to live in our own country"

The mill on the hill

Lagrasse street

Forest walk above Lagrasse

View of Lagrasse from the hills

Charlemagne's foot made this hole in the hills around Lagrasse according to legend – not totally convinced but that's what the locals say it is, so that's that!

The river Orbiere that runs through Lagrasse

The view to the Pyrenees from the hills around Lagrasse

Wild poppies and thistles field

A local vintner's van

Misty vines

The sexiest tree in Lagrasse

Wandering gaucho arrives in Lagrasse with friend

NEARBY CITIES AND TOWNS

Carcassonne castle

Yet another advantage of living in the Aude is we are never too far from one of France's great cities and, conveniently, their airports. In the Cote d'Azur, it's mostly just the airports of Marseille and Nice that provide access to that part of France, but here in the Occitanie we have half a dozen airports within easy reach and many reasonably priced Ryanair routes available to us. We live just over half an hour from the cities of Carcassonne and Narbonne, an hour from Beziers and an hour and a half from Montpellier, Toulouse and Perpignan which means as well as having easy access to their airports we have been able to explore and enjoy their sights and sounds. They are all definitely worth a visit as each offers something different in style and atmosphere whilst at the same time sharing a common heritage.

Carcassonne is in fact a UNESCO World Heritage Site and is famous for its walled fortress called the 'Cité', the largest of its kind in Europe. Said to be the inspiration for the castle in Walt Disney's film animation Cinderella, the fortress is the second most visited attraction in France after the Eiffel Tower in Paris. Hell in the summer due to hordes of visitors and marauding gangs of Japanese tourists barging past everyone photographing everything they see (including their meals) but great fun out of season, it boasts a plethora of gift shops, restaurants, bars and hotels but also pretty squares and alleyways that lead to turrets, towers, a fine Gothic cathedral and even a dungeon.

Carcassonne castle horses – not sure they are very impressed with their owner's choice of headgear

Actually, although the interior part of the Cité is very old, the impressive surrounding walls themselves are the result of restoration work carried out in the late 19th century by Viollet-le-Duc and give the place its fairy tale appearance. The earliest known occupation of the site dates from the 6th century BC when a hill fort (oppidum) was built. It has seen Romans, Visigoths, Cathars, Huguenots, Arabs and the French nobility who all enjoyed the defensive protection of its strategic position on this rocky spur overlooking the valley of the Aude, until of course another would-be owner kicked them out. The citadel includes the Château Comtal, the central castle of the upper town. Constructed in the 12th century, it has over thirty towers, and its best features are the vast rose windows and bizarre gargoyles. It also boasts its own basilica and even an amphitheatre.

Sue, Lucy and Grace recently escaped from the dungeon in Carcassonne

Carcassonne kids!

Below, in the shadow of the citadel, lies the town itself, which also dates back to the Middle Ages. Known alternatively as 'La Ville Basse' (The Low Town) and the 'Bastide Saint Louis', it features bars, shops, cafés and restaurants and is the perfect antidote to the tourist attraction that towers above it. When you drive through and around the Bastide, you will find yourself wondering what all the fuss is about. From the wheel of a car, the inner city appears rather ordinary and even scruffy, but the best advice (which goes for most French towns and villages) is to find somewhere to park up, and go and explore the place on foot. If you do, you will be rewarded by leafy squares and narrow streets lined with quirky shops and bars. We particularly like the little square 'Place Carnot' which is surrounded on all sides by cafés and restaurants; our favourite being Chez Félix where a glass of wine is cheaper than a café crème and, to let you into a little secret, is also Kate Mosse's favourite haunt.

The bestselling author Kate Mosse, most famous for her Languedoc Trilogy (Labyrinth, Sepulchre and Citadel) inspired by the history of the area, lives in Carcassonne. Her books have sold in their millions worldwide. When they made the film version of Labyrinth in 2012, they used our little village to shoot some of the scenes; most memorably the ones of the dead body in the river and another of a horse galloping at full speed over the oldest bridge. The horse had to be shoed with rubber horseshoes to protect it against the cobbles. Apparently John Hurt, one of the stars of the film, upon visiting Lagrasse expressed a desire to buy a house here but unfortunately we never got to see him hamming it up in any of the restaurants. Kate Mosse's lesser-known spooky novel "The Winter Ghosts" is well worth a read on a cold, foggy winter's evening. It is set in the remote gorges and valleys of the wild Ariège region to the west of the Corbières, providing a suitably atmospheric setting for such a magical book.

Narbonne is a friendly, bustling old Roman city that counts among its many attractions a fantastic indoor food market, the Cathedral of Saint Just and Saint Pasteur dating from 1272 with its vaulted choir that soars to over 40 meters, the Canal de la Robine running through (which links up with the Canal du Midi and the Aude river) and hidden gems of quaint squares with fountains and an outstanding treasure trove of art and paintings in the Palais des Archevêques (the Archbishop's Palace) with its 'donjon' and views over the nearby hills. The exhibition of modern north African art on the top floor is most impressive. Narbonne was founded by the Romans in the second century BC and it became the capital of Southern Gaul. At the time it was a major port, although it now lies well inland. The city was built on the Via Domitia, the first Roman road in Gaul, connecting Italy to Spain and remains of the road can still be found in the city centre. It also has its own archaeological museum (Musée Archeologique) and the spooky Roman Horreum, a former grain warehouse built underground as a secret passageway (cryptoporticus).

Carcassonne

Although a workaday place, its atmosphere is one of a large-scale village with plenty of students and young people thronging the pretty streets and wide promenades, lending the city a vibrant and youthful feel. The wrought-iron and glass indoor food market known as "Les Halles" was built in 1901 and opens every single day of the year (including Christmas Day) with the busiest times on Sunday and Thursday mornings.

The sheer quantity of fresh produce on sale is overwhelming;

the fish stalls make up an entire corner of the market where a positive cornucopia of cold-blooded aquatic vertebrates is available to purchase and the range of types, sizes and colours is just mind blowing. Dotted around the fruit, vegetable, cheese and wine stalls are various bars/cafés which are great fun to stop at. You can have a drink or even eat your lunch here. One of the bars, a favourite with the locals, is owned by an ex-rugby player. He orders your meat from the butcher opposite who then throws it to him to catch over the heads of the lunchtime crowd so he can slap it onto the grill! Alternatively, if you wish, you can take home a ready-made meal from stalls selling whole spit roast chicken, paella or North African dishes, like lamb couscous and tagines (if you've not come across a tagine before, it's a spicy, slow-cooked Maghrebi meat dish named after the conical-shaped, earthenware pot in which it is cooked and is a blend of sweet and savoury flavours).

Narbonne market tomatoes

133

Narbonne

Nearby Béziers is similar in style and ambience to Narbonne but is slightly larger and more populous (around 70,000 inhabitants). It too has its medieval cathedral and covered market but also boasts a wide, tree lined boulevard (Allés Paul Riquet) that runs through the centre of the town and hosts the local flower market each Friday. Like nearly all the major cities and towns of the south west of France, Béziers is rugby mad and the Stade de la Méditerranée plays host to many national and international games.

Montpellier is, for me, the most beautiful city in the region with its white stone houses, the towering Saint Clément aqueduct and clean streets with impressive boulevards and squares, especially 'Place de la Comédie' and its Opera House. This is the 8th largest city in France and also the fastest growing mainly due to its ever-expanding population of students. In fact students make up nearly a third of the population of over half a million people. The University of Montpellier is one of the oldest in the world, founded in 1160 and both Rabelais and Nostradamus studied here. The Musée Fabre hosts some truly impressive works of art and makes for an excellent visit.

Montpellier

The city of Toulouse is known as 'la ville rose' (the pink city) due to the pretty colour of its buildings. Like many of the other cities in the region it is sited on an ancient Roman settlement and a lot of the smaller streets remain true to their Roman precedents. Renowned for its spaceflight and aerospace industries with over 35,000 of the inner city's 400,000 inhabitants employed within them (Airbus Group is the largest employer in the region), Toulouse is France's fourth largest city. Straddling the wide Garonne river, it contains many impressive mansions and hotels with the magnificent 'Capitole' as its town hall. As befitting the gruesome history of the area, the legend goes that the Capitole is located on the spot where St Saturninus was martyred. The bishop was said to have been tied to a bull's legs which was then made to career down the steps of the

Capitole, shattering the unfortunate saint's skull open. Charming. The Henri IV courtyard and gate survive from the original medieval buildings and it was in this courtyard that the Duke de Montmorency was decapitated after his rebellion against Cardinal Richelieu. Plus ça change.

These days, the large outside space has been pedestrianised and is generally the first place tourists head for, with its cafés and restaurants commanding an agreeable view of the Capitole and allowing for the obligatory people-watching. The interior of the Capitole houses not just the administrative centre but also a theatre, opera company and even a symphony orchestra. The Salle des Illustres boasts many impressive 19th century works of art.

Toulouse – Capitole

We haven't yet spent as much time as we would like exploring this intriguing city. My neighbour used to work there and says she prefers it to Montpellier and, as we know, the French are invariably right! So, I look forward to spending more time there, wandering the narrow, Roman streets and alleyways, enjoying the restaurants and sight-seeing, perhaps with a knowledgeable French native in tow as my guide.

One of the fun things about living in the Corbières is that you are never too far away from an authentic Spanish paella. Our village is just an hour and a half's drive from the Spanish border and the delightful coastal resorts of Roses and Cadaques are well worth a visit (how can you resist a town called 'Roses'?). The nearby city of Figueres, where Salvador Dali was born, is certainly recommended (although try to go out of season as it gets very crowded in the summer) and it is here that you can visit the splendidly surreal Salvador Dali museum. Most people's favourite installation is The Mae West Room based on his 1934 painting 'Mae West (Face of Mae West Which Can Be Used as an Apartment)'. You have to take it in turns to climb up a stepladder in order to gain the intended perspective. Great fun. Also don't miss the opportunity to visit the tiny jewellery museum at the end of the tour which contains some of Dali's lesser known but most exquisite creations.

Dali's tribute to Mae West

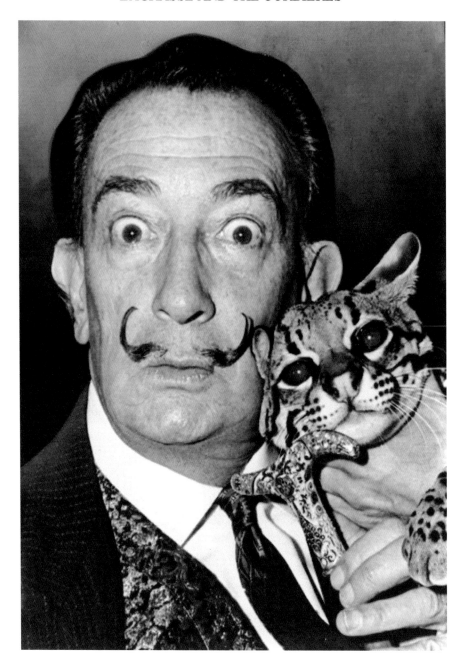

One or other of them is Salvador Dali

The Salvador Dali museum in Figueres

The leaning tower of Figueres

RENNES-LE-CHÂTEAU AND THE MYSTERY OF THE HIDDEN TREASURE

The Devil

A great day out is a visit to Rennes-le-Château deep in the heart of the wild Corbières. The panoramic view from the village is absolutely breath-taking. The area is notorious, not just for its wacky legends, but also for its beautiful scenery, with jagged ridges, deep river canyons, rocky limestone plateaux and large caves hidden away underneath. Castles situated in the surrounding area were central to the clash between the crusaders of the Catholic Church and the Cathar devotees at the beginning of the 13th century. Whole communities were wiped out during the campaigns of the Catholic authorities who succeeded in ridding the area of the Cathar 'heretics' during the Albigensian Crusade (more on that in the next chapter).

This small hilltop village is internationally renowned for being the centre of various conspiracy theories concerning the location of buried treasure supposedly discovered in the 19th-century by its eccentric parish priest Bérenger Saunière. No-one can agree on what this treasure actually consisted of and the sheer diversity of conflicting theories is spectacularly mind-boggling. These range from whatever it was the Visigoths managed to ransack from Solomon's temple in Jerusalem (the ark of the covenant or the Holy Grail perhaps?) to a stock pile of the gold of the Knights Templar or, even more fancifully, the discovery of the remains of Mary Magdalene. She is said to be buried somewhere in the area after supposedly travelling to this region after the crucifixion, either with or without Jesus (his twin brother is purported to have taken his place on the cross and, as indisputable proof according to conspiracists, there are two statues of the baby Jesus in the Sanctuary of the village church). Allegedly, Mary Magdalene was pregnant with Jesus's child upon arrival in the south of France, leading to yet another theory that the Son of God's bloodline has continued unbroken to this day and, therefore, the heir to his throne is alive and kicking as I write; presumably to be found shopping at Waitrose for bread, fish and sandals. The local authorities are fed up with treasure hunters arriving in droves often under cover of the night and proceeding to dig the village up; others wearing helmets with head torches and armed with pickaxes scour the caves dotted throughout the landscape, whilst a few, more intrepid Indiana Jones's have even detonated explosives in the surrounding hills in search of the elusive 'gold'.

The conspiracies centre around the tiny village church dedicated to Saint Mary Magdalene; it has an extremely complex history, having been rebuilt several times. The earliest church of which there is any evidence has been dated to the 8th century. However, this original edifice was almost certainly in ruins during the 10th or 11th century when another church was built upon the site, remnants of which can be seen in Romanesque pillared arcades on the north side of the apse. This survived in poor repair until the 19th century, when it was unexpectedly renovated at great expense by the local priest, Bérenger Saunière. Surviving receipts and account books belonging to Saunière reveal that the renovation of the church, including works on the presbytery and cemetery, cost 11,605 Francs (around £110,000 in today's money) over a ten-year period between 1887 and 1897. The source of the priest's wealth is still the subject of lively debate.

One of the new features he included during the renovations between 1887 and 1897 was the Latin inscription '*Terribilis est locus iste*' above the front doors, taken from the Common Dedication of a Church, which translates as: "This is a place of awe". The rest of the dedication reads "this is God's house, the gate of heaven, and it shall be called the royal court of God."

Just inside the entrance to the church, one of the more alarming additions by the radical Saunière was the figure of an exceptionally nasty looking devil holding up the holy water stoop – a rare though not unheard of addition found in French churches of this particular style. Its original head was stolen by person or persons unknown in 1996 and has never been recovered; so if you ever come across a hideous, dismembered devil's head staring back at you from a mantelpiece somewhere in the world you'll know where it came from.

Saunière also funded the construction of another structure nearby, again dedicated to Mary Magdalene. Named after his favourite saint, he built the Tour Magdala (Magdala in point of fact

Breath-taking view from Rennes-le-Château

**Latin inscription "Terribilis est locus iste" above church
entrance**

means 'tower' in Hebrew) on the edge of the village which he used as his library; it is sited on a belvedere that connects it to an orangery. The tower also has a promenade linking it to the Villa Bethania, which Saunière claimed was intended as a home for retired priests. Account books belonging to Saunière reveal that the construction of his estate, including the Tour Magdala and Villa Bethania (and also including the purchases of land) between 1898 and 1905 cost 26,417 Francs (another £250,000 in today's money). Where did all this money come from?

Tour Magdala

Treasure hunters believe the clues to the location of the so-called 'treasure' were concealed by the priest in cryptic messages within the paintings, murals and frescoes on the walls of the church. Secreted in the images depicting the twelve Stations of the Cross, which are dotted around the interior of the church, is supposedly a treasure map showing where the loot is to be found. Father Saunière unearthed the Knight's Stone with its decorative carvings during excavations and, if the treasure hunters are to be believed, found not only a pot of gold but also a human skull punctured by a hole. Spooky! He may also have discovered mysterious documents enigmatically stashed in a Carolingian pillar and coded inscriptions on headstones. One of the more outrageous suppositions by conspiracists is that there lies a coded message in the inscription to be found above the devil's head which reads *"Par ce signe tu le vaincras"* meaning 'By this sign you will defeat him'. This has been imaginatively reinterpreted so as to reveal a hidden message: there are 22 letters in the actual sentence and 22 letters in the Hebrew alphabet – so if you take the word 'le' as being the 13th and 14th letters of the sentence, this clearly points to the year 1314 which was the date of the execution of the Grand Master of the Order of the Templars. It's obvious really!

There's an even more fanciful legend that, instead of finding your run-of-the-mill 'pot of gold', the priest had in fact unearthed the bones of Jesus Christ himself, meaning of course that Jesus didn't die on the cross, and it is just conceivable that Saunière tried to blackmail the Vatican. The supposition is that the source of his wealth was in fact the Catholic Church authorities who may have chosen to pay off the priest to keep the discovery secret. After all, the Vatican had also historically sought to denounce the possibility that Jesus and Mary were lovers (actually if Jesus was indeed a real person he is most likely to have been a Rabbi and most Rabbis were married). Some believe that, in the 4th century, the Catholic hierarchy rewrote the 'good books' to suit their version of events by assimilating the disciple Maria Magdalene with the prostitute Mary of Bethanie, sullying her good name and thereby debunking the possibility that Jesus was not the Son of God but instead just an ordinary Rabbi in a romantic relationship. Bones of Jesus? Somewhat far-fetched surely?

This and other wild conspiracy theories grew out of various interpretations of a fictional book that the French author Gérard de Sède published in 1967 named *"L'Or de Rennes"*. Following this, another French author, Pierre Plantard, teasingly sold the ideas therein as non-fiction hinting that the oldest French family, the

Merovingian dynasty, was descended from Jesus Christ and that the secret had been kept under lock and key for centuries by a shadowy, secretive organisation called the Priory of Sion amongst whose alumni were allegedly Leonardo da Vinci, Isaac Newton, Nicolas Poussin, Claude Debussy, Victor Hugo and Jean Cocteau. The Merovingian dynasty also featured in the popular book *"The Holy Blood and the Holy Grail"* published in 1982 and the Priory of Sion material later probably gave rise to some of the ideas behind Dan Brown's best-seller *"The Da Vinci Code"* in 2003.

The village received up to around 100,000 tourists each year during the height of popularity of Dan Brown's blockbusting novel "The Da Vinci Code". In this book he continued the theme of the descendants of the bloodline of Jesus and Mary Magdalene still being alive today. Two of the three authors of "The Holy Blood and the Holy Grail" took him to court recently for allegedly plagiarising their work but Dan Brown was acquitted. The third co-writer of "The Holy Blood and the Holy Grail" is Henry Lincoln, an English author, television presenter and scriptwriter who wrote a series of books and several documentaries for the BBC on the mysteries surrounding Rennes-le-Château. His more recent book published in 1997 entitled Key to the Sacred Pattern: The Untold Story of Rennes-le-Château is a recommended read wherein he explains how five local landmarks, when joined by lines on a map, unnervingly create "a sacred landscape, marked out and seemingly venerated by our remote ancestors. Marked out, moreover, with a skill and with an expertise that we, their 'enlightened' descendants, did not suspect they possessed." If I understand Lincoln correctly he offers up the claim that when these five equidistant landmarks are drawn together on a map they form a five-pointed star shape which happens to mimic the orbital pattern of the planet Venus (which coincidentally is the planet most associated with Mary Magdalene). Lincoln however does not engage himself with conjecture of any sort during the book, making clear that he is offering scientifically provable facts only: which I feel lends welcome gravitas and integrity to his work.

The plot thickens though when he mentions a painting by

Nicolas Poussin "Et in Arcadia Ego" (also known as The Arcadian Shepherds). Poussin painted two versions of the subject under the same title; his earlier version, painted in 1627, is kept at Chatsworth House in Derbyshire, England. The range of hills in the background resemble the ones around Rennes-le-Château (you may even be able to imagine a similar landscape glimpsed within one of the paintings in Saunière's church). It depicts three shepherds examining a tomb whilst a mysterious woman looks on. Could the tomb have really existed and did it once house the relics of Jesus and/or Mary? What is known is that Poussin probably visited the area around Rennes during his lifetime and, remember, was subsequently named as one of the alleged Masters of the Priory of Sion.

'Et in Arcadia Ego' – Nicolas Poussin

The translation of the phrase Et in Arcadia Ego is "Even in Arcadia, there am I", the common interpretation being that "I" refers to death, and "Arcadia" means a utopian land but, as I have already stated, other more inventive contributors have propounded the theory that it implies the bodies of either Mary Magdalene and/or Jesus himself are buried in the area depicted. Expounding on this dubious theory we meet the tenuous hypothesis that Mary was pregnant when she sailed from the Holy Land to the south of France and that consequently a bloodline from Jesus and Mary Magdalene exists to this day. The Merovingian dynasty and the Priory of Sion, the latter supposedly including Leonardo da Vinci and Isaac Newton amongst its adherents, are both linked to the myth. However Henry Lincoln is much less interested in this kind of fantasy story-weaving and insists that only reliable, provable facts are expressed in his book and, to be fair, if he makes a conjecture he always makes it clear that the reader should understand these are merely his own speculations.

Henry Lincoln is still very attached to the village and area around Rennes-le-Château; in fact I saw him there myself once recently wandering around the village like a white bearded sage of old, chatting with visitors presumably explaining his take on the more interesting aspects of the mystery. The drummer from the punk band, The Damned, the delightfully named Rat Scabies, is also enthralled by the place and I can recommend his book Rat Scabies and The Holy Grail for a more unconventional angle on the whole saga.

To conclude, it is known that in 1910 the controversial priest Bérenger Saunière was summoned by the archdiocese to appear before an ecclesiastical trial to face charges of trafficking in masses, was found guilty and was subsequently suspended from the priesthood. Typical of his contrary personality, when asked to produce his account books he refused to attend his trial. Could it be that after all the speculation and conspiracy theories his wealth was derived simply from a good, old-fashioned con job such as selling masses illegally by mail order? Regrettably we may have to conclude that this was most likely the case. Still, who cares about the truth? It's way too boring! Let's leave the conspiracists to their theories and hope that one day they do indeed unearth a great secret and a pot of gold to boot.

CATHARS AND CASTLES

In harmony with the light-hearted feel of this book I will not bore you, gentle reader, with an in-depth analysis or detailed, academic re-telling of this most enthralling period of local history, generally referred to as 'The Albigensian Crusade'. If you want to know more about this subject you have only to 'google' it or dive into one of hundreds of books detailing the gruesome fate of these most unfortunate believers. I'll try to offer a simplified, more personal perspective on this macabre phenomenon and its grisly outcome.

Who were the Cathars, these infamous nonconformists of the 12th and 13th centuries and what did they actually believe in? Well, in the eyes of the Catholic Church, they were wretched heretics who had to be wiped off the face of the earth, but for the vast majority of the incumbent Languedociens I imagine they were thought of locally as peaceful and harmless members of their communities. In fact they were commonly known as the 'Good Christians' and the word cathar is said to derive from the greek word for 'pure'. They believed that the world was not the creation of a benevolent god but instead dreamt up by an evil demiurge, and regarded all matter and flesh as corrupt and a source of only suffering. Given the great hardships the local populace experienced in medieval times, the theory might well have seemed attractive and reasonable. Instead of agreeing to be ruled by any worldly authority such as the Catholic Church, which represented only hypocrisy to the Cathars, they were instead believing of a good god who ruled over the non-physical, spiritual world.

Like many religious adherents they too believed in reincarnation; their goal was to live a 'perfect' life and become saints thereby being reborn as angels rather than as ever-suffering human beings. They treated men and women as equals, thought marriage worthless and were accepting of non-procreative sex outside marriage (although they themselves were strictly celibate). They were pacifists, ascetics (fasting was a major part of their religion), believed money to be worthless and refused to take oaths in anything they did not accept as true. This latter forbearance will surely have contributed to their inevitable destruction as they were all eventually killed or burned alive for their unwillingness to convert to another faith or to disavow their own. They were not vegetarians as such but instead eschewed any by-products of the reproduction process and so avoided eating meat, cheese, milk, eggs, butter, and so forth but were happy to drink wine and eat fish (by way of explanation, fish were understood by medieval people to be asexual and spontaneously generated in water).

It interests me to make the comparison with Buddhism and I am not the first to do so. The Buddha taught that every living being is equal in that we all want to be happy and free from suffering. He taught the 'Four Noble Truths': firstly that life on Earth is pervaded by 'true suffering' (our bodies are the source of much of our pain for instance) and that the cause of this suffering is karma (actions and their effects) calling this 'true origins'; he also taught that by following 'true paths' (his 84,000 teachings on moral discipline, patient acceptance, wisdom and compassion, etc.) living beings could attain 'true cessations' (a permanent end to suffering). Buddha also taught that we are all reincarnated and have had countless past lives; he advocated the way of loving kindness. All of which chimes neatly with Cathar beliefs.

Simon de Montfort

On a practical, everyday level, the Cathar movement would seem to have been a counter response by ordinary French people to the corruption and cruelty of the Roman Catholic Church and an attempt at a more peaceful way of life based on tolerance and pacificity, which makes their ensuing total and complete annihilation by the Catholic crusaders all the more shocking. The first major massacre of the premeditated genocide took place in the city of Béziers on 22nd July 1209 when Simon de Montfort, surely one of the cruellest men in history, embarked on the extermination of up to 20,000 men, women and children and which astonishingly took place within a single day. What it must have been like to have been trapped within the city on that day and victim to such a brutal onslaught is almost unimaginable. Death by sword must surely have been the most predominant method of dispatch which would have made for an extremely violent and bloody spectacle. Béziers was burned to the ground on the same day as a final insult.

Simon de Montfort was under orders from Arnaud Amaury, the Abbot of Cîteaux, who was the military leader of the crusaders during these first stages of the purge. It was he who allegedly uttered the infamous words "Kill them all. God will know his own". Charming.

The town of Bram today

153

During the campaign a great many other outrages were perpetrated. At Bram, a small town to the west of Carcassonne, further atrocities were summarily carried out. At the end of the attack on the town, a hundred of the surviving Cathars had their noses and lips cut off, and both eyes gouged out except for one man who had only one eye removed. He was then put at the front of a long line of blinded men and women and was forced to lead them, each joined to the other by a hand on the shoulder of the one in front, back to the castle base of Lastours as a demonstration of the "mercy" of the Catholic church.

The good people of Carcassonne were next in line for the chop. Although well-fortified, Carcassonne was still vulnerable and teeming with Cathar refugees. The crusaders arrived on 1st August 1209 and the siege did not last long. A week later the assailants had cut the city's water supply, which proved decisive. The castle lords tried to negotiate but were instead taken prisoner and Carcassonne capitulated two weeks after the siege had begun. Its people were not killed en masse as before but were forced to leave the town naked "in their shifts and breeches".

Cathars being expelled from Carcassonne in 1209

Simon de Montfort was then chosen as leader of the crusader army and was granted control of the whole area around Carcassonne, including the neighbouring towns, and in the autumn of that year other further flung towns also surrendered, this time without their occupants putting up any resistance.

Later, at strongholds such as Lastours and Minerve, the local lords, who were sympathetic to the Cathars, tried in vain to hold out against further assaults by the unrelenting crusaders. Once the cities had surrendered, the incumbent Cathars were entreated to disown their heretical faith and convert to Catholicism. Many did, but the die-hards died very hard indeed. A hundred and forty of the faithful were burned alive at the stake in Lastours and a similar number met the same shocking fate at Minerve.

Lastours (Cabaret)

The village of Minerve, the historic capital city of the Minervois, is perched high on a hill some 50 kilometres north-east of Carcassonne. Surrounded by deep-cut gorges on all sides, it must have presented a real challenge to the crusaders who sought to root out the Cathars who had escaped from the massacre at Bram, but within a month Minerve had surrendered after a heavy offensive. The Cathars within were given the opportunity to convert to Catholicism, which, as I have already stated most did, but the hundred and forty stalwarts who refused were marched along the still extant Rue des Martyrs before being burned alive at the stake in the gorge below. Minerve's gruesome history is hard to believe if you're lucky enough to visit and stroll round this pretty village filled with art galleries and restaurants where the only burning that goes on is the sunburn the tourists might fall prey to on a summer's day. Amazing day out – well recommended.

The conflict saw many more sieges, including those of Lavaur, Saissac, Muret, Les Casses, Puivert, Toulouse, Marmande, Castelnaudary, Beaucaire and Montségur. Many castles were involved in the fighting, including Fanjeaux, Castelnaudary, Foix, Le Bezu, Coustaussa and the eminent 'Five Sons of Carcassonne' – Pcyrepertuse, Quéribus, Puilaurens, Aguilar and Termes.

Minerve

Château de Termes

Château d'Aguilar

Château de Quéribus

Château de Puilaurens

The Castle of Montségur is famous as the last Cathar stronghold and fell after nearly a yearlong siege in 1244. Near the foot of the hilltop castle, in a field known locally as the 'prat dels cremats' or 'field of the burned', a large and symbolically important massacre took place. More than 200 Cathar Perfects (the religion's priests) were burned alive in a giant pyre, having refused to renounce their faith. The castle ruin is open to the public, as is a museum in the nearby village of Montségur.

Château de Montségur

Gradually, but inexorably, the Inquisition rooted out the remaining Cathars of the region over the next hundred years leaving behind a wake of pain and suffering. As already mentioned in a previous chapter, the last known Cathar Perfect in the Languedoc, Guillaume Bélibaste, was executed at Villerouge-Termenès (just 20 minutes from Lagrasse) in the autumn of 1321.

Trebuchet "bullets" being recovered in the 1960's at Montségur

LADS' WEEKENDS

Five go mad in France!

Since buying the house I have instigated the annual tradition of flying over for a long weekend with a handful of my best mates from our village in England to watch the six nations rugby union clash between England and France on the telly in the local café. Before we leave, my friends' wives often ask their errant husbands, "If the match is taking place at Twickenham, why then are you all flying off to France to watch it?" Well, the honest answer is, of course, that it's an excellent excuse for a boozy, gastronomic weekend away with the lads.

Amazingly, England have beaten France every year since the tradition began, except for 2014 when our flights were cancelled at the last minute due to a French air traffic controllers' strike. Whenever we arrive and sweep into the café, the proprietor, Thierry, throws his arms into the air in a gesture of great despondency and exclaims France are doomed again. His mood is always tempered however by the knowledge that we will be eating plenty of cassoulet and seriously depleting his stock of beer.

I think 2015 was the best of these visits due to the fact we had arrived on "Super Saturday" when the rugby authorities had decided to stage the final three games – Wales v. Italy, Ireland v. Scotland and England v. France – on a single day and so from 2 o'clock onwards we were treated to a veritable banquet of rugby concluding in a fantastically exciting English victory (although the six nations trophy that year went to Ireland on points). There were twenty-seven tries that day which must have been some kind of record and certainly enhanced our enjoyment of the occasion.

In the past, my friends and I would normally stand at the bar to watch the match and naturally celebrated each England score with the traditional loud cheers that famously accompany any important televised sporting event back in England; but in marked contrast to the French customers who would simply clap politely whenever their team scored, which obviously surprised us. On this occasion however, we were the ones sitting down at the tables as a party of forty young French people had converged on the café to celebrate someone's birthday and drowned us out with their own cheering and spirited shouting. Oh well, we still won the match.

The most hilarious lads' weekend was definitely the first trip out back in February 2010. We had a full house on this occasion because Dave, Will, John and Kev all accompanied me on this particular trip. Dave and Kev would have to "Eric and Ernie" together in one of the double beds on the top floor so it was a bit of a squeeze (although their only complaint was each other's snoring). I had decided to offer the lads a rare opportunity to dine on lobster on the first night (obviously an expensive option so this was a special treat for all of us) at a favourite restaurant called La Table du Pécheur in the picturesque, hilltop village of Bages, some forty minutes from the house, overlooking one of the Étangs on the coast. The very best lobsters had already been pre-ordered by me by telephone from England before our arrival, and the owner of the restaurant assured me he would procure the biggest and freshest lobsters at the market on the morning of the event: and he certainly didn't let us down.

**We always swing by Carcassonne castle
for our first aperitif on a lads weekend**

It was some consolation to me (if not the lobsters) that the chef preferred to despatch the creatures <u>before</u> submerging them in the boiling water of the pot, which is the most common method for cooking this particular delicacy in these parts. Otherwise, I'd have felt like former President Francois Mitterrand who famously indulged in the frowned-upon eating of "ortolan", a tiny songbird renowned for its delicious taste and eaten whole after being drowned in Armagnac. Following a hunting ban, the bird was in effect forbidden to be eaten but this obviously didn't deter the Head of State, who with a gathering of close friends at his last meal before his death in 1996, was said to have consumed the head, bones and body in a single, steaming mouthful, while covering his own head and face with a large, white napkin to enhance the flavours. Indeed, Mitterrand was said to linger over not one but two ortolans in his last supper, also consuming three dozen oysters, foie gras and a capon for good measure.

Unfortunately, for one of our party, the opportunity to eat his lobster was going to be missed but earlier on in the day he was not to know that. Kev (originally from Liverpool and still retaining a strong Scouse accent) was perhaps the most excited of all of us to be away on a lads' weekend, so upon arrival on the Friday, after we had unpacked our suitcases and made up our beds ready for the weekend, he and Dave thought it a good idea to wander off from the house and partake of a few beers at the local café. Not realising that French beer can be pretty strong they tucked into a goodly number of "barons", which is French for pints (almost no one in France orders "barons" by the way, knowing full well a "demi" or two is normally sufficient to do the trick) and chatted away amiably to the café owner, and presumably anyone else who would listen to them, for a whole afternoon.

Later on, when it was time to leave for the restaurant, we bundled everyone into the MPV hire car and tootled off to Bages for our meal. Kev had nodded off to sleep on the journey and, when we arrived and parked up outside at the restaurant, he woke up exclaiming he was in no fit state to go anywhere and asked if he could just stay in the car for a short time as he was feeling "slightly unwell". So we left him there and entered the restaurant to be greeted by the infamous Philippe, our waiter who, it has to be said, was more than just in touch with his feminine side being camper than Liberace on a pink pill, and were escorted to a large table overlooking the lagoon, the table being decorated with any number of incredibly over-the-top, kitsch "artistic creations" of shells, bottles and glass containers filled with tiny pink stones, which Philippe proudly assured us he had made himself. To cap it all off, the tablecloth had been sprinkled with bucket loads of red and gold glitter making the whole scene sparkle like something out of a fairy tale.

Having polished off our delicious starters (without Kev of course) I thought it best to pop outside and tell Kev that the lobsters would soon be served and he should come into the restaurant now, only to find him asleep snoring away in the back seat, having not unreasonably emptied the contents of his stomach on the side of the pavement. Not quite knowing what to do, I decided to leave him in peace and headed back into the restaurant.

Soon the lobsters arrived at the table, beautifully prepared, and served by the ever attentive Philippe, who, seeing that Kev's chair was still vacant, became flummoxed and enquired what he should do with Kev's lobster. We apologised sincerely and asked him to just leave it on the table and concluded that there was only one thing for it: we would all have to share Kev's lobster between us as it would have been a crime to let it go to waste or, worse still, after all the chef's hard work, request a doggy bag.

When we had finished our lobsters (and Kev's), the time came for Philippe to clear the empty plates but he was nowhere to be seen. After a period of time, he appeared clutching an iPhone, looking most perturbed, and sidled over to me, grovelling apologetically, and confided to our party that he was extremely concerned for the gentleman asleep in the car because the engine was running and that meant there was every chance of Kev asphyxiating on carbon monoxide fumes that, according to an internet search Philippe had just made on Google, were more likely than not seeping into the interior of the car via holes under the chassis. Highly unlikely, but I thought it best to check on Kev if only to put poor Philippe's mind at rest. Naturally Kev was just fine and snoring away but even so I thought it was time to revive him and after shaking him awake he said he would join us shortly. Kev did in fact manage to resurface just in time to eat his pudding, which by the way was possibly the best course of the evening: offerings of artistically detailed "food paintings" representing the étang and garrigue with blue curacao sauce for the sea and sprigs of herbs for the garrigue.

So poor old Kev's first and only opportunity to eat lobster went begging and to this day he never lets us forget that we ate it for him.

La Table du Pécheur dessert

It is always party time in Lagrasse

A TRIP TO THE
CHÂTEAU OF PEYREPERTUSE

On yet another of our many lads' weekends, Dave and Kev courageously agreed to accompany me on a day out to visit one of the most atmospheric 'Cathar' castles in the far south of the Corbières: the ruined fortress of Peyrepertuse. Perched 800 metres up, straddling a steep, rocky crag, it makes for an awe-inspiring sight. Its name comes from the Occitan for 'pierced rock' and was built in the 11th century. The lower part of the fortress was built by the kings of Aragon and the higher part by the French King Louis IX after the area was annexed to France.

Unthinkable to set off without first reserving a great restaurant for lunch, so we asked around for a recommendation and Josef the artist (who has a knack for signposting a decent eatery or a good wine that springs from years of selfless trials and errors) suggested we opt for the Auberge du Moulin, tucked away conveniently at the foot of the castle in Duilhac-sous-Peyrepertuse. We were not to be disappointed. Located in the centre of the sleepy village, the Auberge turned out to be the perfect resting place after our morning visit to the castle.

After an hour's picturesque drive through the rocky garrigue on the winding, narrow roads of the Corbières, passing through Villerouge-Termenès, the site of the infamous burning alive of the last Cathar priest Guillaume de Béllibaste, skirting the hills around the chateau of Termes and cruising bemusedly passed the wonderfully named village of Davejean ("Is it just the two of them that live there?" said Kev from the back seat), we decided we were in need of refreshments. On the approach to the castle we stopped off for morning croissants and steaming cups of good, strong French coffee at Cucugnan, just a couple of kilometres from Peyrepertuse. Cucugnan featured in the short story, "The Priest of Cucugnan", published in 1869 by the Parisian author Alphonse Daudet in his collection Letters from My Windmill. Daudet's story is based on a sermon by the Abbot Ruffié which attempts to persuade the local Christian congregation to turn to a virtuous life by recounting an imaginary trip to heaven, purgatory and hell, where the narrator finds all the old inhabitants of Cucugnan being tortured among the flames. Quite what they had done to deserve this was to our eyes unclear. Everyone we met seemed perfectly friendly and utterly blameless. Letters from My Windmill was eventually adapted as a film by the famous French film producer, Marcel Pagnol.

The mill at Cucugnan

Feeling suitably reinvigorated we returned to the car and resumed our journey. From here it would have been possible to visit the other notable 'Cathar' castle in the area, that of Quéribus, but destiny, in the guise of a wrong turn I made, led us instead directly

Château de Peyrepertuse

169

to the chateau of Peyrepertuse and our fate was sealed. Soon the castle materialised majestically above us and from down below, the fortress appeared to morph out of the surrounding rock making it impossible to tell where the rock ended and the castle began; the whole a quixotic blend of magic and reality, like something out of a dream.

Peyrepertuse looms overhead

Following our instincts, we drove up and up until we could go no further. We parked in the rough, gravelly car park and began our walk up to the castle, only to be met by at least a dozen Morgan motor cars.

Must have been a Morgan club outing – very impressive, though somewhat incongruous considering the location. The steep climb on stones worn smooth by thousands of previous intrepid explorers led us through enchanting woodland with tiny glades to stop at along the way to catch our breath. You could just imagine the castle dwellers of centuries ago making the same trek perhaps with their livestock or carrying provisions up to the stronghold overhead. We kept a lookout for any Cathar ghosts hiding behind the trees along the way and were met instead only by tourists scrambling back down the hillside having already visited the caste. One jocular Frenchman we met on his way down asked, "Are you looking for the castle?" to which we replied in the affirmative and he quipped, "I wouldn't bother if I were you – there's only half of it left!" Très drôle.

**Unexpected sighting of Morgan motor cars
at top of Peyrepertuse**

One of the wonderful things about this part of France is that we're pretty sure they don't yet have a translation for 'Health and

Safety'. The drop over the side on the walk up, and once we had entered the castle, was interesting to say the least, with no attempt by the authorities to detract from the fun of it all by erecting warning signs or barriers. Great for us strapping fifty year olds but plenty of older visitors we met up top, who were not so sprightly on their feet, definitely found the experience somewhat daunting. Once inside the walls, we realised our friendly Frenchman we had met on the way had been right and there really was only half a castle left, with few ceilings in the various rooms and antechambers remaining but the view was absolutely stunning.

Spectacular view from the top of Peyrepertuse

With the odd dungeon and a fabulous, now open-air chapel with its single nave, semi-circular apse and views of the castle of Quéribus, the tower of Far de Tautavel and Força Real in the Roussillon to the south, we found the whole experience most atmospheric. The chapel was called 'la Chapelle Sant-Jordi' which understandably brought cries of "wey aye, man!" from Dave and when I pointed out the rock-strewn floor Kev commented, "they've really let the place go – could have swept up!"

Window seat with view

View of the castle below from the Chapelle Saint-Jordi

**A long way down from the recess of the Chapelle
– "they could've swept up!"**

Kev, still recovering from his fear of heights, was keen to get back to the car and admittedly Dave and I were beginning to experience the first rumblings of our empty stomachs, so bidding the wonderful ruined fortress of Peyrepertuse farewell, we all traipsed back down the path, salivating at the thought of the Auberge du Moulin tavern awaiting us patiently in the little village below in the valley. You will probably laugh but on the way back down the magical, dreamlike trail, I had the strangest feeling that I had once been a child in a past life, centuries ago, skipping and playing along this pathway.

The view to the Pyrenees in the south

View of village of Duilhac in the valley below Peyrepertuse

Auberge du Moulin

And so, to lunch at the Auberge du Moulin in the delightful village of Duilhac-sous-Peyrepertuse below the castle.

Alfresco dining at the Auberge du Moulin

Not knowing what to expect, we were delighted to find a quintessentially French setting for the most eagerly awaited part of our trip. Nestled between the old windmill and the village's beautiful stone houses, right in the centre of the village, the Auberge appeared before us like an oasis. We made our way across the already busy terrace and sat outside at a corner table, sheltered from the hot sun by green, leafy trees and with a commanding view of the valley. Then, as modern blokes do, proceeded to get our mobile phones out and check for emails and texts. Well, the restaurant owner was having none of it. When he came over to take our orders and we asked him first of all whether there was any WI-FI or internet connection, he promptly picked up our three phones and dumped them at the end of the table, declaring: "Here no 'Wee-Fee' only whisky!" Fantastic. We laughed our socks off.

The fireplace at the Auberge du Moulin

After some swift aperitifs of cold beer for Dave and Kev, and an ice-cold glass of Muscat for me, we ordered our food and wine. As I've stated before, you can almost always rely on the house wine in this part of France and, at a fraction of the price of a bottle, it's very good value. So we ordered a large pichet of red which turned out to be delicious. The wine came from the nearby village of Maury and I thoroughly recommend it. Here's a tip: buy it in the box, either 5 or 10 litres, and you'll save a fortune. Just as good as many of the other fine wines around, at a fifth of the price.

Our entrées were soon served up and were an absolute delight. The lads had chosen swordfish tartare with fresh, local tomatoes and I'd opted for local goats cheese wrapped in aubergine and red peppers accompanied by thyme-flavoured ice cream. Unfortunately for us, the wild boar option was not available and so, for the main course, we all opted for grilled lamb chop flavoured with local herbs accompanied by roast onions and new potatoes. This proved to be a perfect decision – they were truly unforgettable. To finish, we indulged in a chestnut panna cotta, an almond slice with figs and a local delicacy of fromage frais with strong honey and pine nuts. The obligatory café / cognac rounded off a simply perfect meal. Many thanks to the 'whisky not WiFi' man!

Rogues gallery at the Auberge du Moulin

Before wending our way back to Lagrasse, we took a detour to experience the famous Gorges de Galamus. Not for the faint-hearted, the drive consists of two kilometres of what are called 'balcony roads' which are so narrow in places that only one car at a time can negotiate them and you find yourself reversing round a few blind bends to let other cars pass. At the centre of the Fenouillèdes massif, near the towns of Saint-Paul-de-Fenouillet and Cubières-sur-Cinoble, just over the border from the Aude in the Pyrénées-Orientales, the gorges with their steep drops and winding hairpin roads make for an exhilarating ride. You can stop half way and grab an ice cream at a tiny café open to tourists close to a small hermitage built into the rocks. Surrounded by mountains, the views are spectacular with the cliff walls dropping hundreds of feet into the gorge below. We were told in the café that the road had been built by men attached to ropes. Not a job I would have volunteered to do!

Gorges de Galamus balcony road

**Canyoning in the Gorges de Galamus
(for this and other thrill-seeking activities, check out the
website: www.oxygen-aventure.com)**

Suitably chastened by the power of nature at its most magnificent, we tootled back home to Lagrasse at a leisurely pace through the quiet countryside having thoroughly enjoyed our little adventure and vowing to return soon to this magical part of the Aude to visit more of its famous Cathar castles.

Hermitage Saint Antoine in the Gorges de Galamus

AND FINALLY...THE FRENCH!

Much has been written on the character traits of the French people, as individuals and as a nation, so I will not attempt to outdo my fellow quill-drivers here, except just to share with you, in a light-hearted manner, some of my own personal experiences. After all, we are all individuals and we all have vastly differing personalities and it is hopeless trying to generalise when it comes to a national identity. Even so, with their long history and broad culture, the French people, on the whole, can be said to be a proud and strong-minded bunch, with a penchant for fairness and social equanimity;

hence their national motto "Liberté, Égalité, Fraternité" which found its origins in the French Revolution, of course. An intelligent and philosophical nation with great centres of learning like the Sorbonne in Paris, France is today the sixth most powerful country in the world and can boast many accomplishments. For me, the high quality of their gastronomy certainly stands out as being one of the most admirable skills that they possess. My French friends tell me that it stems from being geographically close to so many other countries in Europe, which has allowed French cuisine to be influenced and enhanced by other great cultures over time.

Nevertheless (and I'm sure you must have encountered this as well) why is it that whenever I mention the French to people back in England, the stock response is invariably negative? Most Brits seem to think the French are arrogant, unhelpful and rude, demonstrating a smug confidence in their superiority alongside an intense Gallic pride. I guess that, for instance, certain ingenious articles published in the media about the "exemplary" behaviour of French children or on why French women don't ever get fat, will have only helped to reinforce this impression. However I think it has more to do with a communication breakdown as, let's face it, only a handful of English people can string a sentence together in French. How can one expect to understand others' motivation or their personalities without understanding what they are saying?

Furthermore I think people forget sometimes that the English are an exceptionally or, dare I say it, overly polite nation. In the south of Europe, the locals do not tend to bother with niceties. For instance, the Spanish rarely need to say please or thank you, the Italians are well-known for their unswerving, vocal appreciation of attractive women and the French are certainly direct in their approach when asking for something. You don't often hear the French using such terms as "may I…" or even "je voudrais…", as we are often 'over-taught' in schools in England; they just state the object they wish to procure and get on with it. So if a Frenchman wants some bread, he simply says to the shopkeeper "une baguette". Perhaps it is this directness that the Brits confuse with arrogance or rudeness?

Admittedly, from time to time, the French can seem, shall we say, somewhat dismissive. The wonderful, colloquial exclamation "BOF!" (meaning loosely "I disagree", or even, "whatever") is often levelled upon hearing any, even mildly, ill-considered statement or sentiment, the French preferring to go at a discussion from a more negative angle than most and gradually work their way up to a conciliatory "oui" or "d'accord". I sometimes wonder if their favourite word isn't "NON!". The former President of France, Charles De Gaulle (who once said: "How can you govern a country which has 246 varieties of cheese?") certainly played his part with his infamous retort of "non" when Britain wanted to join the common market; and who can forget the rousing Edith Piaf song "Non, je ne regrette rien"? Georges Brassens, the famous singer and poet (born up the road in Sète near Montpellier) trumped them all in his song 'Le Bulletin de Santé' with "non, non, non, trois fois non" (no, no, no, three times no!). So if you enjoy a rumbustious, good-natured argument, then France is certainly the place to be.

As I've mentioned previously, driving in France is an absolute delight, with its bowling-green motorways and well maintained 'routes nationales' (the quality of roads in England is a disgrace in comparison), and the French take on driving etiquette is also very different. On the roads in England, drivers constantly feel it necessary to thank one another with a wave, a smile or flash of the headlights whenever someone gives way to them. I suppose I shouldn't disparage this well-meaning national habit, as it makes for a gentler experience and must help to reduce road rage; but I do get fed up worth it, especially when you even have to thank the other driver for thanking you! Occasionally, a French driver will acknowledge another's thoughtfulness with a wave of a hand, but in general the French don't bother to stand on such ceremony, preferring to just get on with it and, when necessary, jostle for position on a first-come, first-served basis (Italians behind a wheel are notoriously boorish and often don't feel the need to use their indicators when changing lanes, as anyone who has driven around Milan or Naples will know). Still, it's damned annoying when French drivers choose to drive as close to your car's rear bumper as is physically possible, especially on the narrow, winding roads of the Corbières hills. Off-road, the French behave in a similar way to when they're driving; forget forming an orderly queue in shops or at a bar as this is anathema to the French. Only the English ever complain "there's a back to this queue!"

I do have to admit a frustration with France's love affair with industrial strikes. I've lost count of the number of flights I've missed due to cancelations following French air traffic controllers' walkouts. Obviously it can work both ways: there were times when I was glad to be 'forced' to stay in France for a couple of extra days due to a strike but of course it can also be an annoyance, like when the lads and I had to miss a flight out for a rugby weekend at the last minute. Recently, in 2016, President Hollande (nicknamed 'Flanby' by the French after a pale, wobbly custard as a result of his ineffective and weak brand of politics) uncharacteristically decided to play hardball with his people by attempting to lay down a new law making it easier to hire and fire employees and force them to work longer hours. He was met with an almost unprecedented series of strikes right across the country with planes, trains, nuclear power stations, petrol depots and petrol stations all greatly affected and either shut down or blockaded. I had to cancel business meetings and postpone the drive back to England because, at the time, half of France's petrol stations had no petrol. The French obviously do not like being told what to do by their authorities. One only has to look back in history at the 1968 Paris riots, Napoleon's antics and the chopping off of heads during the Revolution in the eighteenth century to be reminded of the French people's intransigence and obduracy when it comes to the state telling them how to behave.

One thing however that we Brits have in common with the French, apart from the bulldog spirit when faced with adversity (the French rugby union team never play more convincingly than when they have been written off by the press or their supporters) is offering a cheery good morning or "bonjour" to every passer-by. In fact the French go one step further and often offer a handshake upon entering a café or bar – even to strangers. Yet another endearing act that sets the French apart from their close neighbours is to kiss one

186

another on both cheeks upon meeting – even the men!

The busiest time in France is early in the morning with markets and shops closing at noon for two hours so everyone can enjoy the great highlight of French culture – the long lunch. As I've already mentioned in a previous chapter, one of my most cherished memories of life in France (when I was a teenager spending each summer with a French family on an exchange visit) is a lunch in the countryside which lasted six hours. Grandparents, parents, children, cousins, nephews and nieces were all present and in between the many courses the children would run off and play in the garden whilst "les grand-mères" prepared, cooked and brought out the next dish. It has to be said that unfortunately this practise of long lunches is becoming less and less of a feature of modern-day French life, especially in the cities, due to the time constraints of business and the ever greater preponderance of fast food. I have recently read for instance that the average time spent eating lunch in France is just 25 minutes. Still, if you look hard enough, especially in the countryside, you will still find French families indulging in this fabulously enjoyable experience.

In my humble opinion, France has the most beautiful countryside, the most exciting, cosmopolitan cities, and the greatest food and drink in the world. I also believe that the French people have the best understanding of how to enjoy life to the full. Sure, they have at least twice as many days of sunshine a year than the UK which allows them to enjoy alfresco dining and a café society, but it is the people themselves that create the renowned "high quality of living" culture. So maybe us Brits should rethink our attitude towards them, try to look a little deeper into the French psyche and finally (grudgingly) give them the respect they deserve? Rant over.

BIBLIOGRAPHY
RECOMMENDED READING

Stephen O'Shea, The Perfect Heresy – The Life and Death of the Cathars, (Profile Books Ltd.)
A popular history of the infamous "Good Christians" – the best of many books about the Cathars.

Stephen O'Shea, The Friar of Carcassonne – The last days of the Cathars (Profile Books Ltd.)
More about the Albigensian Crusade.

René Weis, The Yellow Cross – The Story of the Last Cathars (Penguin History)
More horrible histories.

Sean Martin, The Cathars, (Pocket Essentials)
Yet more on the hapless heretics.

Henry Lincoln, Key to the sacred pattern – The untold story of Rennes-Le-Chateau (The Windrush Press)
The link between a famous painting by Nicholas Poussin and the landscape of Rennes-Le-Chateau reveals a mystery stretching back thousands of years.

Michael Baigent, Richard Leigh and Henry Lincoln, The Holy Blood and the Holy Grail (Arrow Books)
Did Jesus really die on the cross or did he and Mary Magdalene escape to the Corbières? Is a descendant of Jesus Christ alive today? Controversial and great fun.

Daniel Start, Wild Swimming France, (Wild Things Publishing)
Rivers, lakes and waterfalls of France – wonderful photographs and accurate, extensive mapping of the best swimming spots.

Richard Peace, Cycling southern France – Loire to Mediterranean, (Excellent Books)
Enlightening guide to the best cycling routes.

Brian Catlos, The Rough Guide to Languedoc and Roussillon, (The Penguin Group)
Comprehensive and extremely helpful guide to the area.

Rosemary Bailey, Love and War in the Pyrenees, (Phoenix)
Thought-provoking account of the exodus from Franco's war-torn Spain during 1939-1944.

Rupert Wright, Notes from the Languedoc, (Ebury Press)
The journalist Rupert Wright's take on the Languedoc.

Kate Mosse, The Winter Ghosts, (Orion)
Spooky, atmospheric novella by the author of the Labyrinth trilogy set in the foothills of the Pyrenees.

Angela Murrills, Hot Sun Cool Shadows, (Raincoast Books)
Savouring the food, history and mystery of the Languedoc.

Genevieve, Merde – The real French you were never taught at school, (Simon and Schuster New York)
Brilliant compilation of everyday French language as it is really spoken with plenty of slang and 'gros mots'.

The author in his natural habitat

About the Author

Stuart Benton fell in love with France at the tender age of twelve and has worked with French people and French companies all his adult life. Recently, after visiting the deep south of France, he took the plunge and bought a house in a medieval village. Since then, he has been ferrying himself, his family and friends back and forth in the vain attempt to persuade them all to emigrate with him. He was born in Shropshire England, is married with four children and didn't vote for Brexit.

Printed in Great Britain
by Amazon

57068348R00111